About the Author

Rob Frowen was born in Blackpool and has lived there most of his life. Mainly a civil servant in his working life, he also received a medical degree in 1989. He has written many articles for magazines and edited his own publications. He took early retirement to care for his son, Christopher, who has enduring mental health problems.

He was awarded a United Kingdom Carer of the Year award in 2017 in recognition of his caring and charitable efforts.

He continues to undertake voluntary, charity work and campaigns for carers' rights. He also contributes regularly to radio programmes. He lives with his second wife Sue.

Email: robertsfrowen@gmail.com
Twitter: @FrowenRobert

The Long and Winding Road
An unmapped mental health journey

Rob Frowen

The Long and Winding Road
An unmapped mental health journey

Olympia Publishers
London

www.olympiapublishers.com
OLYMPIA PAPERBACK EDITION

A CIP catalogue record for this title is
available from the British Library.

ISBN: 978-1-80074-194-2

First Published in 2021

Olympia Publishers
Tallis House
2 Tallis Street
London
EC4Y 0AB

Printed in Great Britain

Dedication

For my children, Hannah and Christopher, who have given me
endless inspiration and determination to write this book.

INTRODUCTION

For more than 45 years Rob Frowen and I have been acquainted — and it has been a pleasure and privilege to know him. We have each travelled our separate 'long and winding roads' through the many phases of our often, parallel lives. Throughout all of these phases so far, his insightful, committed, sensitive and caring nature has guided him through the many challenges he has faced along the way. This book is about just one of them — but the biggest — and most long standing by far.

I have known Rob as a fellow civil servant, a good friend, family man, single father, football fan and entrepreneur, magazine editor, HUGS carers' group leader and charity fundraiser for The Carers Centre and last but not least, as the absolutely unconditionally committed carer for his son, Christopher. It was for his caring role that Rob was awarded United Kingdom Carer of the Year by the Marsh Christian Trust in 2017.

Rob and I have a lot in common — starting in the early 70s with the Civil Service and more recently both having the primary caring roles for our much-loved sons. We are both able to appreciate the positives of any challenges this responsibility brings: a good day and a single achievement being magnified a million times!

I believe Rob's philosophy to be similar to mine. As carers and as individuals we have each grown to be as resilient as we are, fully able to achieve goals and to help others with theirs. Such successes have not been 'despite' the responsibilities we have had for our sons, but I believe, 'because' of them, and the overwhelming love, joy and inner strength that those we care for can bring us.

I wish Rob and his family every success in the future — and know we will all learn a lot from his book — about caring, about his life and those around him — and about our own lives and feelings.

Dr Judith Poole MBE

PREFACE
The Long and Winding Road
An unmapped mental health journey

My son, Christopher James Robert Frowen, was born at 2.08am on Sunday 20 March 1988 in Blackpool Victoria Hospital. Chris's mum and myself had arrived at the maternity unit only a few minutes earlier at exactly 2am. It was, therefore, immediately apparent to us that Chris was in a considerable hurry to begin his life adventure. And he seems to have been in one heck of a rush ever since! Read on and discover the reasons why this is the case.

The title is an appropriate choice because my son and I have battled together through a veritable morass of twists and turns in the last dozen or so years since his first hospital admission. Chris's complex mental health issues have presented us with huge challenges but we have always been in this together for the long haul. That is, until our long and winding road has reached its happy conclusion. We have had to contend with so many obstacles on the way and we will continue to overcome them for as long as it will ever take. My prime objective in life is to see my son freed once and for all from the mental health problems that have beset him for so long and I am confident that we will achieve this aim in the end.

I have written the book entirely through the perspective of a carer. It is a journey that chronicles the considerable range of challenges, emotions and fears that have accompanied my role as a carer and as a father. I make very few clinical observations because this is not my field of expertise. The same applies to technical information with regard to mental health matters so I also keep these to a bare minimum. This is the story of our roller-coaster ride through so many testing and rocky times, although I hope you may come across occasional flecks of humour which are interspersed here and there.

There are a number of varied reasons for my writing of the book. The idea came to me soon after the start of the Covid-19 lockdown which, as I'm sure most of you will be well aware, began in March 2020. I shielded for my wife, Sue, and continued to do so for the full twelve weeks. She has a lung condition and is included within the category of the 'most vulnerable' people in the country. It was vital, therefore, that both of us stayed safe and well out of harm's way at all times. I quickly discovered that I had a large amount of spare time on my hands and I soon arrived at the conclusion that this would present me with an ideal opportunity to take on this venture. It had been on my list of things to do for a good while anyway but the predicament that we found ourselves in finally pushed me over the edge.

This entire writing experience has proved to be very rewarding and cathartic. A problem shared is a problem halved sprung to my mind many times as I wrote. As a regular fundraiser for charitable causes for quite a while I will make a donation to a worthy Blackpool based charity if there are profits from the book. And hopefully, I may be able to set aside something for the benefit of my son, without whom, of course, this book would not have been possible.

I have always regarded caring for my son as a real privilege although the reality of it has often been quite different and has presented many challenges over the years. I am very much a 'glass half full' type of person and prefer to dwell largely on life's positive aspects, whenever it is at all possible. You may notice several examples of these inbuilt traits as you read. I might just add that my optimistic take on life is reflected in a rather excessively upbeat and positive way as far as Chris and his various behaviours are concerned. In the real world it has often been quite different. My wife, in particular, has endured many traumatic experiences during the last decade as a result of my son's ways and actions. In fact, it is something of a minor miracle that she has managed to come through it all relatively unscathed.

My story predominantly focuses on Chris's life since he first became a teenager. It was then becoming apparent that all was not well. What were the reasons for his declining mental health? I include lots of background information, family factors and historical details that date back to Chris's early childhood days. These may help the reader to form a clearer picture of why his early years were blighted with a number of different issues.

Looking back now I could, and maybe should have, recognised a number of warning signs that were yelling that his mental health wasn't all it should have been. I hope that you might pick up one or two snippets of advice and may even recognise early signs of concern in the lives of your own families and perhaps learn from my own experiences. Some of you may have had the misfortune to suffer personally from mental health issues at some stages in your lives and others might be involved in a caring capacity. You will find that my own caring role in the community features strongly in the book.

Sadly, illnesses of the mind appear to be very much on the increase these days. And the mental health legacy that Covid-19 will leave behind us is likely to be of long-term concern to us all. The issue of steeply rising numbers of mental health patients in our country set against a backdrop of ever-reducing services, at a national level, is a worrying scenario to say the very least.

It is a sad but true fact that as many as one in four people in the United Kingdom will experience some kind of mental health problem *each year*. And about one in six people report experiencing a common mental health issue in any given week. It is also estimated that seventy five percent of people in the country may not get full access to the treatment that they actually need. I'm sure you'll agree with me that this is a staggering collection of statistics.

And that's before I even begin to mention the subject of carers. Three in five people in our country will at some time in their lives become carers. The vast majority of care in the United Kingdom is provided by family and friends, who make up a total of six and a half million carers.

I trust that you will find the contents of my book are not 'doom and gloom' laden by any means. Amidst the strain, anxiety and occasionally a little anger that has punctuated our lives from time to time, there have also been many happy times. And sometimes, if Chris ever gets annoyed or irritated, I will say to him, 'for every minute that you're angry you lose sixty seconds of happiness'.

The two of us try to smile and laugh as often as we able to, even in the most difficult of circumstances, and we have found that this provides us with a period of brief respite. You may even have a chuckle or two yourself as you read our quirky, but one hundred per cent genuine, stories that are scattered around amidst the more serious subject matter.

I feel it is inappropriate to mention anyone by name who may be alluded to in the book other than members of my immediate family. This is unfortunate in many ways because so many doctors, nurses, care and support workers that we have come across on our journey have performed their duties exceptionally well, nursing and supporting Chris. They have invariably cared for and acted in his very best interests and, most important of all, that have continued to keep him safe. In my opinion, one or two people haven't fared quite so well, though, and may have failed to live up to expectations. It is perhaps just as well then that this small number of individuals retain their anonymity.

It is not my intention to be controversial with the views and opinions that I express. In fact, nothing can be further from the truth. Everything I have written is designed to be as candid, honest and open as I have possibly been able to make it. This ensures that the dramas, events, situations and even the dialogues to a large extent, are related in the ways that they actually occurred.

My sincere thanks go to Dr Judith Poole who has been good enough to contribute with an excellent introduction and to every single one of you who has helped me on the way to completing this project. There are too many of you to mention individually but you all know who you are. Also, special thanks go to my family, especially my wife, whose constant support, patience and encouragement has proved invaluable throughout.

And finally, I really hope you enjoy reading my book as much as I have enjoyed writing it.

Chapter 1
Three Years Inside and Rising Tensions

'How much longer do I have to be in this bloody place, for fuck's sake!' Chris screamed, bright crimson in the face and with his arms flailing, during an important CPA meeting in January 2020.

The CPA (Care Programme Approach) assembly had gathered around a large, oval-shaped table and included Chris's consultant, his care co-ordinator, a junior doctor and a few of the nursing staff. I could fully understand my son's intense frustration although his dubious choice of rhetoric didn't exactly have me dancing a jig.

Chris's short tirade was met with a response from one of those present and went roughly along the lines of, 'we will be looking at all the possibilities with regard to suitable placements, together with a specialised care package for Chris. We will also be investigating ways of securing the necessary funding that will be required'. The dialogue sounded a little like a broken record as we had grown accustomed to hearing this kind of oration all too often.

I found it necessary at that point to chirp in with a hint of uncharacteristic sarcasm. 'I expect the next thing you'll be doing is to stage another meeting to decide exactly when you can convene yet another meeting after that...?'

This was not especially helpful, of course, but it did make me feel a little better and allowed me an opportunity to let off some steam. The meeting petered out as we reached an unsatisfactory impasse. In the final analysis, the end product amounted to little more than my son being granted an additional half hour's escorted leave from the ward each day. Chris and I had grown accustomed to outcomes like this one but it didn't make the pill any easier to swallow, having to go over the same ground once again.

Tensions ran high and I did my best to keep Chris as calm as possible throughout the meeting. My son is inclined to 'shoot from the hip' when he feels pressure building up in him and his brief explosion was a good example of this. I recognised that if there was a repeat tirade it would do him no favours at all. It might even add to the prevailing opinion that he was far from ready for a discharge from hospital and a return into the community.

Although Chris's mental health was as good then as it had been for some time, we still hadn't heard any news that gave either of us any cause for optimism. For Chris, it was once again a case of a return to the old, miserable hamster wheel. I remember feeling so sorry for him as I saw him trudge haplessly back to the ward and away into his bedroom — or into his dungeon as he was often inclined to call it.

We had done our best (other than Chris's mini outburst) to positively influence those present at the meeting but we could still not see any glint of light at the end of a long, dark tunnel. A good workman cannot perform without the use of his tools is a saying that rings true in this context. The subject of cuts in mental health services all over the country have made the working lives of professional health workers increasingly difficult, stressful and challenging. There are nowhere near enough beds available or adequate numbers of doctors and consultants currently in post to cope with the growing demand for mental health illness in our country.

My son had spent more than half of the last ten years in hospital and he was fast approaching thirty-two years of age. He had spent almost three years 'inside' this time, detained under Section 3 of the Mental Health Act. We were so disappointed that little was happening in terms of either facilitating a constructive therapy programme, a structured rehabilitation placement or even to consider the possibility of a full discharge with imposed conditions, such as having a Community Treatment Order put in place.

A Community Treatment Order is more commonly referred to as a CTO and this allows a person to leave hospital and be treated safely in the community rather than in hospital. One would still be under the auspices of the Mental Health Act even though you could live in the community. But the terms of a CTO also mean that one must keep strictly to certain conditions. The clinician will write down all the conditions that will specifically apply to an individual. If one cannot follow the terms of the Order, one can be made to go back into hospital. It is also possible to be recalled to hospital if it becomes apparent that the person starts to become unwell again.

So I could well appreciate the anger that occasionally boiled over in Chris. I tend to agree with him in many respects — my support for him has never wavered despite a whole catalogue of challenging behaviours that we have all had to contend with. He is prone to acting highly impulsively both in a verbal sense and with his actions. And he tends to react on initial impressions, often giving little thought or consideration to background information or to the wider context of a situation. These are major elements associated with the hyperactive condition ADHD (attention deficit hyperactivity disorder), which has conspired to blight Chris's life since his early childhood. We will examine the condition, and implications which have arisen from it, in much greater detail at various stages in the book.

Chris can present in a buoyant mood on some days. He can be warm, engaging and a pleasure to be with but at the opposite end of the spectrum, he can be gloomy, morose and unpleasant, often for no apparent reason. I feel that it's somewhat like the action of a roulette wheel — one has no idea where the ball is going to land when it comes to a halt and one never knows for certain which part of Chris's character will awaken on any given day. I do not possess clinical knowledge of such complex matters but judging from his many fluctuating presentations, it seems very possible that he suffers from multiple layers of various mental conditions. And these are inclined to spring to life entirely at random which can be challenging for everyone concerned, and especially so for Chris himself.

When Chris was caged into the back of a van on 2 April 2017 in readiness for an eighty-mile journey over the Pennines to a hospital in West Yorkshire I could scarcely even consider the possibility that he may still be locked up on a section more than three and a half years later. He had been living independently in a flat only a mile or so away from where I live and a mere two hundred metres from Blackpool's golden beach at the southern end of the town.

A delegation of two doctors arrived unannounced on that cold Sunday morning to adjudge whether Chris would require a further spell in a mental health unit. In other words, they had to decide whether he needed to be sectioned. One of those doctors was approved under Section 12 of the Mental Health Act and the other was a General Practitioner from Chris's own practice. This is standard practice when situations such as these arise.

They had to make a decision there and then about his

immediate future, eighteen months following his last discharge from hospital. Two police officers also arrived and stood unobtrusively near the door of his flat. They were present as a precautionary measure in case things started to get difficult. Or if Chris had been tempted to attempt 'a runner' and, given his considerable past history in this regard, it was always a distinct possibility. We will visit the subject of my son's colourful absconding activities several times.

The doctors talked amongst themselves for a good while, and then spoke to Chris and myself. The discussions continued for the best part of an hour until they had reached their decision. I was sat in another room with a nurse who also arrived on the scene. She did her best to keep me calm and went through the various options that could happen. I had been involved in a similar situation with Chris previously so I felt reasonably 'in the loop' but it was still comforting to have someone there to act as a distraction if nothing else.

When a decision was reached it came as no surprise to me at all. The doctors had determined that Chris was seriously mentally ill and must to be taken to hospital immediately. A hospital bed had been provisionally reserved for Chris if the need had arisen.

Chris had been sliding into a relapse for a number of weeks and had reached a critical point. The intense activity that day came as a complete shock to Chris; he reckoned that he was still in pretty fair shape, mental health-wise, and failed to understand what all the fuss was about. I'm positive that he was the only person present — and that probably includes anyone who had come into contact with him in recent weeks — who couldn't see what was blindingly obvious to us all.

It was back on Bonfire night 2015 that Chris continued his life of freedom in this newly decorated flat on the same day that he had left hospital. An excellent package of care had been set up to help him adjust to life on his own. An organisation known as Next Stage Limited was drafted in to offer Chris the help and support that he would undoubtedly need in those vital early weeks and months. Their staff would visit him several times each week and take him out to various places in the area and help him adapt to being in the outside world. These people did a fine job helping him with his daily jobs and guided him into safe areas. They did occasionally have to contend with some very challenging behaviours but their patience and tolerance held together admirably.

Next Stage's mission statement states that 'the organisation has provided care and support to vulnerable adults since 2002. Their drive and ambition is to be the best provider we can be, which is a reflection of how well we can assist those who need care and support to improve their own independence and quality of their own lives'.

This organisation sounded just the ticket for Chris and we all looked forward to working together as one big happy team, sharing identical goals and ideals. The support from the Next Stage team was available to Chris from Monday to Friday and they did their utmost to engage him in activities, courses and voluntary work within the limits of their thirty hours a week support. This should have been exactly what we had waited so long for but Chris had other ideas and decided not to take up many of the opportunities that were made available to him. A significant barrier to his stubbornness was the use of cocaine, which he had sadly renewed his interest in not long after being discharged. We will look at Chris's cocaine habit and the problems it has caused for him in greater detail later on. He was encouraged to engage with *Inspire*, a community drug and alcohol service, as it became crystal clear that his drug use was leading to a high level of boredom. He attended Inspire's group therapy sessions once or twice but felt it was doing him no favours at all, as he was inclined to express it. Inspire is a drug and alcohol service which provides all aspects of drug and alcohol treatment with aims to promote recovery from addiction and dependence.

Several months later, after Chris had made very little progress, a decision was made for Next Stage to continue with their same level of support but with 'more realistic goals'. Everyone hoped that a vital breakthrough may still be possible but it was starting to look much less likely.

Next Stage continued to do their utmost to engage him in activities but with little to show for their efforts. Chris eventually grew tired of their visits and, as he said in his own words, 'I'm sick of these people coming round here and interfering in my life'. It was clear for all to see that this was the beginning of the end. Everything was visibly crumbling.

The relationship with Next Stage was finally dissolved after a couple of bad incidents had occurred, one of which involved Chris becoming a little heavy handed with a member of their staff. Their support was duly withdrawn, partly for the above reason and partly because Chris was telling anyone who was prepared to listen that he 'didn't need them coming around to see me any more'.

Their departure from the scene meant that our own next stage was a case of the two of us back on our own again. His decision to terminate the relationship with Next Stage ultimately turned out to be very costly indeed for Chris.

Returning briefly to 2 April 2017, this proved to be the final day of Chris's freedom, at least for his immediate future. I have to admit that it was myself who had instigated the mental health assessment that day. His care coordinator and myself had been locked in extensive discussions for several days trying to fathom out the most effective way of handling the worsening situation. We both seriously feared for Chris's personal safety and for the safety of others that he might come into contact with. So we mutually agreed to set up this Sunday summit as we dared not run the risk of leaving it even a day longer.

Despite the fact that the doctors had clearly made the correct decision on that spring morning it was still unbelievably sad for me to watch my dazed and confused son, clutching tightly to his favourite teddy bear, as he was guided into a special vehicle that was ready and waiting to take him to West Yorkshire.

The scene in the car park that morning represented a huge paradox for me — I felt incredible relief that my son was now in safe hands again at long last and I would be able to sleep soundly for the first time in ages. But my release from fear and worry was tempered by the haunting sadness of the heart-breaking image I was left with.

We now fast forward three years (although I'm sure that for Chris it was anything but a fast three years) and his recent journey has taken him to no fewer than a staggering twelve hospitals in four north of England counties. And despite our relentless pursuit for a solution to his long-term detention we are still waiting for the day when he can finally be released. Chris remains on his section, although he is in far better mental health than he was even a year ago. It was then that he had been earmarked for discharge from his section and primed for a move to a facility in nearby Lytham St. Annes. The place is called 'UBU', an acronym which means simply 'You Be You'. It is a highly respected care provider for people who have complex needs and varying degrees of learning disabilities. It was looking very promising at one stage but eventually the move did not come to fruition. We will learn more details about this aborted mission in chapter seven.

His prospects of release after the UBU setback then looked as uncertain as ever. It has been said by many people over the years that Chris is very much 'his own worst enemy' in terms of how he conducts himself and handles his behaviours. I also subscribe to this view but only to a limited extent because I have always maintained that he is controlled to a large extent by his multiple conditions.

Chris's mental health issues are considerable and wide ranging and he is undoubtedly a highly complex individual. And I'll be the first to admit that he has been a very difficult patient (I use the term 'patient' because I dislike the expression 'service user' which appears to be the more commonly used term nowadays) for the professionals and other caring staff to handle ever since he first became seriously mentally ill in 2009. It has not been an easy ride at all for anyone involved in the process of caring for and nursing him. Let it be suffice to say, at this stage, that Chris has travelled along on a rocky and uneven road ever since he was in junior school. And that road ahead was destined to become a good deal rougher once he reached his teenage years.

Chris landed at his new hospital, which is situated a few miles away from Bradford, and I received the perfunctory telephone call from a staff nurse shortly after his admission to confirm that he had arrived safely. He was allocated a warm room, and apparently felt so comfortable that he quickly fell sound asleep. And I was able to rest a whole lot easier as well.

He rang me on his mobile during his first evening. The staff had fortunately allowed him to keep hold of his device which was invaluable to him for many reasons including accessing YouTube for his favourite music and for playing games. The policy in some hospitals can involve the temporary confiscation of mobile phones when a patient has newly arrived until they are considered to be more settled. In some facilities mobiles may also be taken away because the act of taking photos within the wards is strictly prohibited. This prevents patients from forwarding images on to friends and family — or maybe posting photos on social media platforms. Phones may be reset by specialist staff and returned to patients afterwards minus their ability to take photos.

Chris spoke about the painful journey over the M62 motorway as it dawned on him that he was moving further and further away from home. He moaned for a little while about how he was unable to talk to anyone while he was in transit but we chatted on quite merrily for nearly an hour. In fact, he sounded so upbeat and chirpy that it felt to me as if he was away on a day trip somewhere and would be returning home again later on.

The hospital is situated in a semi-rural location and set in beautiful, large, scenic grounds and in a tranquil setting. Chris would have seen the spring tulips and daffodils splashed all around the landscaped gardens as he arrived up a steep driveway although I'm sure that attractive and colourful flower displays would have been far from his thoughts then. And that is presuming that he was able to see much at all through the grills of his cage.

His room was on an 'acute level' ward and it was pleasing to learn that he settled in quickly. An acute ward is characterised by, and available for, people who are in a crisis, when care cannot be adequately provided in their own homes.

I'm sure that Chris appreciated the calm and controlled atmosphere that a peaceful ward brought him. It must have come a great relief for him to have left his Blackpool flat and all the associated carnage behind.

In the tranquillity of his new room on the ward, there was no longer a need for him to consider whether to tidy up his messy flat, or to hunt around for something to eat, to attend to his laundry, or to worry about any of his unpaid bills. He didn't even need to think about whether or not he might decide to take his daily medications because all these things were now being taken good care of.

Chris's mental health had gradually deteriorated over a number of months and other tenants in the flats told me that he had become 'a bit of a nightmare' with his noisy and riotous behaviour. Music had apparently blared out very loudly and crashing sounds were heard in the middle of the night. They regularly complained to me and I fully empathised with their annoyance. I eventually had to resort to tiptoeing up the concrete staircase to avoid meeting anyone on my way upstairs. And, to cap it all, a large opaque glass door panel at the ground floor's main entrance was repeatedly shattered. No one ever owned up to being responsible for the damage but I think everyone had a pretty fair idea who the culprit was.

Chris had become almost out of control and fluctuated between being in manic states and then deep in the depths of despair. His flat was usually in an awful state and I had to 'blitz' the place tidy almost every day to make it anything resembling a habitable state. I pleaded with him to keep the place tidier but this tended to fall on stony ears. To all intents and purposes, I became his daily cleaner — a regular bucket, brush and mop guy! Seriously though, I tried everything I knew to stem the tide of psychosis that was threatening to overwhelm him. He would often sleep for most of the day and at night too. I secretly feared the day that I would arrive in the morning and be unable to awaken him. I made a point of checking on him at least once each day as it became increasingly evident that he was close to a return to hospital.

I visited him in his first week in West Yorkshire along with his care coordinator who offered to drive me the eighty miles in his car to facilitate the visit which I gratefully accepted. He worked wonders for Chris and we were so grateful for his admirable efforts on his behalf. He also helped me with so many mental health issues during his time with us. I aimed to emulate the way he dealt with difficult situations and managed to remain calm. Sadly for us, he moved on to take on a fresh role elsewhere.

I established a rapport with the helpful nurses there and also with the ward manager and was invited to attend regular meetings with his consultant and ward staff to discuss Chris's care, treatment and recovery plan. I travelled each week to the hospital, sometimes with my daughter, Hannah. She was always keen to cheer up her brother and to add her views and knowledge at the meetings. It's very often said amongst the mental health carers' fraternity that families are more familiar with patients' general traits than anyone else. And I am a very firm believer in this. I would never dream of making recommendations of any kind with regard to clinical matters. For example, I would never suggest that we should consider prescribing this or that type of anti-psychotic medication instead of the present one. Or recommend that Chris should be tried on a different mood stabiliser as it could prove more efficacious than his current one. But as far as specific behaviours, the history of a patient and key life experiences, we definitely do know best. We were grateful that the senior staff were more than happy to listen to Hannah's and my own views and opinions — and they sometimes even acted on them. This mutual co-operation and support from clinical teams was not always in evidence elsewhere at several hospitals around the north of England where Chris had stayed.

The weeks passed by and Chris had settled in nicely and stabilised very well. It was very encouraging for us all to see his mental state improve so much and the improvement in him was more in evidence each time I visited.

As a result of this positivity, the ward staff decided to grant periods of Section 17 leave with a member of staff who would act as an escort. This section of the 1983 Mental Health Act makes provision for patients who are detained under the Act to be authorised leave of absence from hospital, normally for short periods only. Not surprisingly, the change of environment and scenery outside boosted Chris's well-being and morale considerably. I found that he was in chirpy moods more often and even optimistic about his future prospects during our telephone chats. I'm certain that this was due to the impact his periods of leave were having.

One day, however, whilst he was out on one of his Section 17 leave breaks, he decided, on the spur of the moment, to elude his escort and make a run for it. Chris is a highly impulsive person (one of the unfortunate consequences of his ADHD condition which we will cover in some depth in the next chapter) and he tends to live very much 'for the minute'. He pays scant regard to any risks that may be involved and to the immediate, or longer term, consequences of his actions.

When an absconding situation occurs, the escort is permitted only to coax and encourage the patient to return to the ward and must not attempt to apprehend the patient in any way. However, on this occasion, Chris quickly showed the guy a clean pair of heels as any thoughts of gentle coaxing were quickly rendered purely academic. A chain of processes quickly followed as standard practice in these situations dictate. The ward staff were swiftly notified that Chris had run off. The local police were then contacted and I was told the news and was promised to be kept bang up to date with developments.

This is always a very worrying time for the family, as one can imagine. A thousand thoughts blur through one's mind and these can often be pretty bad ones with so many uncertain outcomes. Notwithstanding my natural tendency to remain positive, there is so much uncertainty that flies around when this kind of situation happens. For a start, Chris was in a town that was completely unfamiliar to him. I pondered for a good while and several questions sprung to my mind.

Could he find himself lost, become disoriented and start to panic?

He might become ill and how would he be able to take his medications?

Could he find himself placed in a vulnerable situation that may be potentially dangerous?

How much money does he have with him?

Does he have warm clothing with him in the event that he decides to stay out all night?

In fairness to Chris, he always rings me, whenever it's possible, to tell me what has happened. He would normally ring me and merely say, 'Hi, Dad, I've escaped again, but I'm okay, so don't worry. I'll keep in touch.'

He kept his calls very short for fear that his location would be traced and he'd likely be swooped upon and caught.

It is clear then that Chris has considerable 'form' and can be justifiably termed a classic 'serial absconder'.

This time, however, it was a somewhat different scenario.

On every occasion that he had made a bolt for it in the past, it had occurred when he was based in his home town, Blackpool, and amidst familiar surroundings. And despite a colourful escapism history that Houdini would have no doubt been proud of, I was still a very worried man. When the Yorkshire police contacted me soon afterwards to seek out snippets of information of his background, it only served to heighten the drama and increase my stress to even higher levels.

A few hours passed uneasily by and Chris was still 'at large'. My imagination was running riot. I conjured up images in my mind, of hordes of West Yorkshire police officers hunting around in ditches or in derelict barns for one possibly drunken or poorly Chris. I have to admit that I gulped down a few stiff whiskies at the time — a very rare event for me especially during an afternoon, but it just had to be done! I would not be called upon to pick him up in my car as I had done many times before when Chris was local and had grown tired of being a fugitive. Maybe he's starting to get weary, or cold, or under the influence of something or other. Perhaps, it's a combination of all of these, I thought. Fortunately, the alcohol had numbed my anxieties — for the time being at least.

I was a couple of tumblers of scotch, two hours further down the line and half sozzled when I received the call from the ward manager that I had prayed for. He had been found, safe and sound, and was in the process of being returned to the hospital in a police car. What untold relief! When I learned later of the exact circumstances which surrounded his discovery and subsequent capture by the police, I could not help but laugh out loud. He was tracked down to a farmer's field about a mile away from the hospital and was spotted innocently stroking and feeding a cow! This shouldn't have surprised me too much because Chris has always loved being with animals and tends to gravitate to them whenever he can. I made a mental note of this for future reference if a similar crisis ever occurred again.

The upshot of all this episode was that he lost his Section 17 leave privilege for the foreseeable future. But by that stage he was well and truly used to all that.

Three months later, Chris was moved from Yorkshire to The Priory at Cheadle Royal in Cheshire. His mental health had taken quite a hit towards the end of his stay in Yorkshire. He told me that he felt trapped and worried that he would remain over there for ever. His way of dealing with the predicament was to be stroppy and rebel against both members of staff and patients alike. As a result, it became necessary to transfer him to their PICU unit in a different part of the hospital. 'PICU' is an abbreviation for Psychiatric Intensive Care Unit. This type of ward is far more secure and everything is stricter, and the risk of absconding is very low. Staffing levels are higher than on acute inpatient wards and usually multi-disciplinary and sometimes with 'one to one' nursing ratios.

He failed to settle even on the calmer environment of the PICU ward. As there was no improvement in his behaviour it was decided that it would be in his own and everyone's best interests if he made a fresh start somewhere else. And so, once a bed became available, he was sent off to a different hospital in Cheshire.

The Priory is a facility that is marginally closer to home than Cygnet but not by any significant distance. My visiting days were still likely to be lengthy affairs. The main advantage for us was that this Priory hospital has an excellent reputation. It is privately run and provides 'innovative, high-quality treatment for patients with challenging and complex needs, in order to enable their recovery and re-engagement in the community'. The extract is from their website and this certainly proved to be very accurate and prophetic in our case.

Chris's mental health and his well-being improved significantly during his three months on their PICU unit. He received lots of therapy, personal attention and some top-class treatment there. The staff kept me bang up to date with news and reports about his progress and rang me regularly. This was a lovely touch which has not been replicated in other hospital wards where Chris has stayed. He told me at the time that the staff there made him feel valued which hasn't sometimes been the case elsewhere either. But all he really wanted to know was the answer to one central question: 'For goodness sake, Dad, when are they going to let me out of hospital? It's been months and months now, and I seem to be getting no further.'

It was close to six months since he had been sectioned and I really didn't know how to answer him. And more than three and a half years later he was still asking me the same question…

The Priory is a private hospital and the substantial cost of his stay was ultimately borne by Chris's home authority, Lancashire & South Cumbria Primary Care Trust. As there is clearly not a bottomless pit of cash in their kitty, he was eventually forced to pack up his bags and it was back on the road for him again. The next move would become his third hospital in just over five months.

It was late September 2017 and the destination was Blackpool, an excursion back home to our roots which delighted Chris. When I was first informed of this move back home to the seaside I was in London. It's very strange but I can still recall exactly where I was standing at the moment he told me the news, almost down to the cracks in the pavement on the Euston Road!

He was bound for the recently-built Harbour Hospital on the outskirts of the town.

Chris's cross-country treks often take him back home to Blackpool and to the Harbour. As far as he is concerned, he feels spiritually much happier when he's back in town and, of course, he has the benefit of receiving more visitors. He was born and bred in the town so who can blame him? One of his favourite sayings is, 'I feel so much happier when I'm closer to my Tower and to Dinky (our cat)'.

One advantage for me, of course, is that the hospital's close proximity makes visiting so much easier and faster. In fact, I could be locking up my bike in the Harbour's car park a matter of just ten minutes after leaving home.

Several hospitals where Chris has stayed in the past have involved full day excursions to visit him and eventually it can become a little tiresome — and tiring too. But if I ever feel a little brassed off about it all I think of the plight of poor families who live hundreds of miles away from where their loved ones are hospitalised. I realise then, that things could be a darn sight worse.

So Chris returned happily to the Harbour Hospital and I guess we all felt largely the same way. But it was at his new place that fresh troubles quickly brewed again shortly after his arrival.

In chapter 7 we continue the story of Chris's marathon North of England Tour from 2017 right through to the present day, together with his many experiences along the way.

CHAPTER 2
OUR FAMILY AND CHILDHOOD TIMES

Christopher's mum and myself first met at a local squash club back in the August of 1985. I was coaching some of the junior players there at the time and she asked if I fancied giving her a lesson. I quickly accepted her invitation and, following a drink afterwards, we seemed to hit it off straight away. I was thirty-two years of age (the same age as Chris incidentally, at the time of writing) and although Judith was still a teenager at nineteen years old, we did have plenty in common and soon began to date regularly.

It was only a matter of five short months later that we were married and Hannah, our first born, was already well on the way. It doesn't take a genius, therefore, to work out a timeline that was involved!

Hannah was born on 25 June 1986 as the football World Cup in Mexico was reaching its climax. It was a scorching hot day and the country was still up in arms about the late Diego Maradona's 'Hand of God' goal for Argentina against England just three days earlier. But football was the very last thing on my mind on that smouldering hot day as I became a father, at long last, shortly after 7pm in the evening.

From the very start it was evident that Hannah was a bright girl and we always thought that our daughter would go far in life and we have been proved right. She was alone with us for twenty-one months until Christopher James Robert Frowen joined us on 20 March 1988 to complete our family of four.

Chris was a robust and jaunty baby and I was thrilled to have a boy; I had one of each now and this was a 'dream ticket' for me. I would have someone to play football with and to watch the local matches with when he was a little older. I wasn't to know then but it was Hannah who was probably the bigger football fan in those younger days.

As events turned out, it became necessary to watch our football team from a considerable distance away because early in 1990, when Hannah was four years old and Chris was just two, we moved as a family to Durham. This change of direction had come about due to a promotion opportunity that arose with my job. We reckoned that if there was ever going to be a good time for such an upheaval it would be then before the children had started school.

It was a happy time, by and large, over there although the winters were far colder than we had been used to. And, of course, we missed our families and friends who were back in Lancashire. The children had hardly ever seen snow before and were thrilled that it was in plentiful supply in County Durham. Secretly, I was quite excited by it as well! A few months earlier, we had purchased a new house on a modern development in a quiet semi-rural area and it was still in the process of being built as I began work in my new role in the north east. In all honesty, the house was far too large for us with four sizeable bedrooms and situated on a large plot of land. I watched the house gradually rise from the ground almost on a daily basis as I stayed in temporary accommodation during the working week, and returned to the family in Poulton-le-Fylde only at weekends.

We took formal possession of our new house in April 1990 and, in the early months, most of our spare time was taken up with home improvements such as decorating, buying carpets or getting to grips with the garden areas, which the builders had left in a bit of a state.

Hannah was old enough to attend reception class at the local village school whilst Chris at two years old remained at home with his mum. Shortly afterwards, one or two indications began to emerge which suggested to us that Chris was developing hyperactive tendencies. He could not stay still for any length of time; he was a veritable whirling dervish and we often found him banging his head against walls when he was in one of his fully charged up moods. It soon became a real problem for us. I returned home from work on a number of occasions to find Judith in a really frazzled state, often complaining that it was the additives in his food that were making him manic and almost uncontrollable. I knew exactly where she was coming from and really sympathised with her. There were many times when I wished that there had been options for me to work evening sessions of overtime in the office!

We realised that Chris may have a real health issue but tended to dismiss the thoughts, laying it down at the time to 'terrible twos' syndrome. We kept our fingers and toes crossed that this was merely a youngsters' phase that might just fade away naturally on its own accord. But things didn't improve and we discussed his problems endlessly in attempts to find out what the reasons actually were.

We considered the possibility that a form of autism might be responsible for the way Chris was behaving and this subject cropped up regularly during our conversations. We speculated that the MMR vaccination (measles, mumps and rubella), for which he had received an inoculation earlier, might be one reason why his behaviour was turning out this way. There was plenty of discussion in our household about the whole subject and, indeed, it was extensively debated throughout the country during that era. The topic triggered all manner of speculation about the safety of the vaccine, and a few of those theories persist even to this day. We eventually decided not to pursue the matter any further because we recognised that if, by any chance, his jab was the reason for the way he was presenting then there was precious little that we could do about it, in any event.

Instead, we began to carefully research the subject of ADHD in children and proceeded to hunt around local libraries for all available literature on the subject. Children with Attention Deficit Hyperactivity Disorder, a condition characterised by inattention, overactivity, and impulsivity, are most frequently identified and treated in primary school. We were surprised to learn that boys are classified with ADHD approximately twice as frequently as girls and primary school age children almost twice as frequently as adolescents. We discovered, many years later, that the condition can also extend in some people well beyond adolescence. ADHD symptoms exist on a continuum in the general population, and are considered as a 'disorder' to a greater or lesser degree depending on various factors. Excessive levels of inattention, overactivity, and impulsivity characteristic of ADHD are present from an early age. Most of the foregoing seemed to fit Chris to a 'T'.

Early signs of ADHD, however, can sometimes have co-occurring other behaviours, such as temper tantrums and aggressive tendencies that may overshadow symptoms of inattention and overactivity and could possibly distort a diagnosis. Once again, this all sounded very much like our Chris.

It would have been extremely useful if the 'google' search engine had been available to us back in 1990 together with the plethora of information that is available now over the internet. It would have helped enormously but we simply had to make the best of what we had at our disposal. We continued to ask ourselves whether it was completely normal for a lad who was still not yet three years old to be so terribly fidgety, ever restless, irritable and constantly bored? We could accept the fact that he had difficulty keeping still for more than a few seconds and unable to keep quiet for more than ten seconds at a time but banging his head on the ground and against walls was clearly not typical behaviour. It worried us a great deal and it was likely that this practice could prove dangerous to his health too.

We decided to take him to our local doctor to receive an informed opinion. He quickly noted Chris's hyperactive presentation and decided to refer him to a specialist in the field. I remember the anxiety I felt that he would present in a calm and relaxed way and the doctor would then look at us in utter puzzlement. But thankfully Chris performed to his usual standards on this occasion and fired on all cylinders!

The specialist quizzed us about Chris's diet and more particularly about sweets and other confectioneries that we were treating him to. He mentioned chemicals such as E110 Sunset Yellow and E102 Tartrazine amongst others, all of which sounded double Dutch but they soon started to make perfect sense to us later. We learned that certain colourings, sweeteners, flavourings and other chemicals that are added to sweets can cause hyperactive reactions in certain susceptible children. It was starting to look increasingly likely that Chris fell into this category. He was prescribed a special diet and had to adhere to it religiously for a period of four weeks. We were to return later and report our findings and look at any options that were open to us. His 'special diet' comprised little more than awful, dry rice cakes and one of two other, less than appetising, treats. But every credit to Chris as he stuck rigidly to the diet so well for the entire period. The experiment, however, did not yield any measure of success in the final analysis. So he had endured a month of eating a wretched, bland diet with nothing at the end of it to benefit him.

We were determined not to give up and, during a further visit, the specialist arranged for Chris to spend a week in hospital to undergo a revolutionary new trial. A month later, Chris checked into the local hospital where he was monitored very closely every minute of the day and throughout the night too. He would be required to eat another unappetising diet. This time is was purely biscuits that was on the menu, and little else, for the entire week. Some of the biscuits were laced with 'e' additives and various other suspect substances whilst others were merely placebo based. The staff observed him very closely for all reactions to the special concoction of impregnated biscuits, with their clipboards ever-present.

I visited him each evening after work and noted that his moods fluctuated wildly. For some reason, I was encouraged by this presentation and prayed that we might be on the right track at last. One evening, late in the week, he was about to be given a bath just as I arrived. His nurse asked me if I would like to carry him into the bathing room for her. I was naturally delighted to oblige and lifted him through, telling him all the time what a good lad he was and how we were so very proud of him. He responded by spitting in my face over and over again! The nurse noted my utter horror at this and whispered to me, 'Tell him what a good boy he is and keep praising him.'

'Is all this completely normal?' I whispered back to her.

'Absolutely. It's purely to be expected. There's definitely a marked reaction to his biscuit diet today,' she replied.

'Well, he's definitely left his mark on me,' I joked.

'Very droll,' she replied, acting as though nothing out of the ordinary had happened.

I continued to tell him 'how good he was' but he continued to spit at me and wriggled around until I was able to lay him gently in the bath.

As I went to the bathroom to clean myself up, I worked out in my mind this whole experiment might be going very well and somehow sensed that the experiment would reach a happy conclusion. We both eagerly awaited the results that would be revealed to us the following week.

The results, however, proved to be a huge disappointment. We were told by the specialist, with the results spread on the desk in front of her, that the entire experiment had proved 'inconclusive'. What it meant in essence was that the biscuits that were designed to make him hyperactive had little effect at all and the placebo biscuits, which should have produced a nominal reaction, had sent him manic once or twice. My first thought, albeit flippant and hardly appropriate, was that I must have caught him during the bath incident after he had just polished off a diet of placebo bikkis!

So we were back to exactly where we started. I'm sure that we were in the same situation as countless other parents who are left to hope that their children will simply grow out of their various issues in the fullness of time. We were advised, in the meantime, to be extra careful when buying sweets or other confectioneries that might seem risky and brightly coloured, especially yellow. We did cut back significantly on his sweets and chocolate treats then anyway and we began to study the wording on packets of food and sweets before buying to check their contents. It is obviously a mainstream policy for shoppers these days but thirty years ago folk didn't seem to scrutinise food labels quite so thoroughly.

We moved back to the north west in June 1993 after I managed to wangle a transfer back with my job and we bought a house in Lytham. We chose this small town, which is close to Blackpool, because we heard from quite a few sources that their schools were of a good standard and, like every other parent, we wanted our children to have the best education possible.

Hannah and Chris were accepted for admission to the local Junior and Infants school and we bought them their smart green uniforms in readiness for the new term which would start in a couple of months.

Chris continued to be hyperactive for a good percentage of the time but we had simply grown to live with it. He wasn't getting any worse in this respect so we thought that was a bit of a bonus. And it didn't seem to bother him unduly when he was on a high. In fact, he appeared to thoroughly enjoy the feeling of being 'hyper' which apparently is a common trait amongst similar sufferers. Things did get on top of his mum and dad now and again but we always managed to come through it all and retain some semblance of sanity.

I feel it's highly relevant at this point to raise an issue which I have long considered to be a major factor regarding Chris's behavioural issues and his fragile self-esteem since he was old enough to walk. His grandma, my mum, always favoured Hannah from the very start and made little secret of it. My daughter had been around for quite a while before Chris's arrival but it was apparent even in the early days after we became a family of four that Hannah was the star of the show and Chris was often cast almost as an 'extra'. Sadly, as the years drifted by the gulf widened even further with the consequence that Chris found himself often marginalised whenever we had family get-togethers, which was pretty often in those days.

My mum was a wonderful, caring person and I have to say that my sister, Julie, and I never wanted for anything whilst we were growing up in Blackpool and we enjoyed happy childhoods. But my mum and I did have this one major difference of opinion. She would tell me so many times over the years that one should always have a particular favourite son or daughter, brother or sister or whatever and this concept was always alien to me.

Hannah obviously didn't mind at all about any of this. In fact, please tell me a six- or seven-year-old child that would be overly concerned about being a favourite child? Chris resorted to gravitating towards me whenever attention was being heaped on my daughter. He must have been confused by it all and it had to hurt, although he never outwardly displayed it. Looking back now, I probably tended to over-compensate when these domestic situations arose and sub-consciously made more of a fuss of him, ostensibly just to level things up and to make him feel just as loved and important.

It didn't occur to me until later — more than ten years later, in fact — that his low self-esteem and the lasting damage it may have caused could be directly linked to his early childhood experiences with my mum. His grandpa, my mum's second husband, whom she married ten years following my dad's premature death, treated both of our children equally and Chris thought the world of him. Sadly, he died during the early weeks of the Covid-19 pandemic and the impact of his death on Chris (and on Hannah too) was considerable and I refer to this again later in the book.

It is widely recognised that young people with low self-esteem are more at risk of developing depression, anxiety, self-harming and other mental health issues as they grow up. Chris did self-harm quite often when he reached his twenties and the subject is covered later. People with low esteem levels can often find that the ups and downs of life can be harder to get through as well. It is also generally considered that unfavoured children act negatively in order to receive attention. They can often think that they are the bad and naughty one because they have heard it so often whilst growing up. The more I think about this, the more it all seems to fit together like it's an integral part of the jigsaw of Chris's life.

Hannah was always well behaved as a child and a pleasure to be with. She was also, of course, the first born and this factor alone can sometimes play its part when the word 'favouritism' ever comes into play. Yes, we knew that Chris could be very hard work at times and was often a little disruptive especially to someone who was, by then, in her sixties but I preferred to love and appreciate him for the person he was and for his uniqueness. I often repeated all of this to my mum but without much success, I'm afraid.

Soon after we arrived back in the north west Chris started to develop asthma and was prescribed an inhaler by his new Lytham doctor. The doctor suggested that the condition could have arisen due to the move from one side of the country to the other and his subsequent return to the north west years later. Apparently, it may have been connected to the slight atmospheric differences between the opposite sides of the country and varying levels of dampness in the air may have also played their part. He also began to develop a stammer quite badly when he was about five years old and we considered the possibility of a course of speech therapy if things hadn't improved.

We were probably justified in thinking that our son had been dealt a rotten hand in life with the handicaps that he had to contend with even up to only five years of age. Fortunately, the asthma and stammering conditions petered out on their own accord during the course of the next year and we were then back to just the one central health problem to deal with.

School life was going pretty well for both children at their new school. Hannah was always happy and as bright as a button and we just allowed her to breeze along to learn in her own merry way. And she was diligent too — forever in her bedroom busying herself with homework and other school projects. Chris was also faring reasonably well during his first two years with the infants. We did, however, receive one or two reports that he had been acting a bit silly and messing around in class but this didn't worry us too much in view of the fact that he was still only very young.

I taught him to kick a football around and we were regular exercisers on the local beach at weekends. My big hope for him was to show some promise and to display sufficient interest to maybe get into his school's football team one day. He was a strong and bustling type of footballer and it was his bite and aggression that finally helped him to be selected for the First XI. He was really thrilled about this because his self-confidence had always been quite low as he felt he always played 'second fiddle' to Hannah. It niggled him that he never seemed to receive the same level of praise and attention that she received. He now had a big chance to achieve something that she wasn't able to excel at. There was also another reason why I focussed so much on his footballing activity. It was to encourage him to burn off lots of excess energy that was always screaming to be released and maybe we could then see a calmer and less irritable lad at home. And a more contented one to boot.

Although Chris continued to impress his classmates with his developing football skills, his school work deteriorated markedly once he reached seven years old. His concentration in class was reported to be virtually non-existent and he seemed unable to focus on his lessons for any meaningful length of time and unwilling, or unable, to learn anything new. It was because of his inability to pay attention in lessons that he was often considered 'off task' and proceeded to be disruptive and play silly pranks.

We knew that the ADHD was most likely responsible for his problems in the classroom but the teachers seemed to interpret that his shortcomings were largely due to poor behaviour. Things continued to worsen until, once again, four years after our last attempts, we sought medical advice about his concentration problems, his irritability and occasional bouts of out-of-control behaviour.

Over the course of the next twelve months Chris met with a whole host of professional people which included educational psychologists, behavioural psychologists and clinical psychologists. They showed a keen fascination in him and the ways in which he presented. But we wanted far more for Chris than him becoming little more than a curious exhibit of interest. The best solution they collectively came up with was to prescribe him a course of Ritalin to see whether that would have the desired effect of slowing him down. Judith and I sometimes formed the distinct impression that we were the ones who were placed under the microscope and may somehow be the ones who were contributing to his behavioural issues.

Ritalin, otherwise known as Methylphenidate, belongs to a class of drugs known as stimulants. It can help increase the ability to pay attention, keep focused on an activity and control behavioural problems. We were warned at the time that Ritalin should be used with caution as the quality of evidence that was available then about both its risks and benefits was poor.

I can't say that we were particularly enamoured by the above rider and we were a little apprehensive to give our permission to trial it at all. But we did eventually agree to give it a go and he was prescribed the lowest of dosages, at least in the initial trial.

Several weeks passed by and we closely monitored his behaviour and concentration but we noticed very few positive changes at all. And we were always nagged by the possibility that there may be long term side effects associated with the drug as it was still a fairly newly marketed product in this country. We decided, therefore, to take him off Ritalin, not least because it didn't seem to be helping his condition at all and he was not becoming any calmer.

At the age of ten, his teachers finally recognised the fact that Chris was struggling badly in class and that it wasn't entirely down to his bad behaviour. Arrangements were consequently put in place for Chris to be assessed by the Education Authority to determine whether he should be given a statement of special educational needs. Such a statement describes a child's needs and any special help that they should receive. As I recall, it was a long, drawn-out process but it eventually resulted in Chris being 'statemented' and deemed, therefore, to require some measure of extra educational help.

As a result of this, an outreach teacher was drafted into school to coach Chris on a one-to-one basis, two or three times a week. He very much appreciated the personal element to his tuition but he would tell me repeatedly that, although it was a welcome break from his regular lessons, he didn't feel that it was doing him very much good at all.

'It's all simple 'Jackanory' stuff, Dad, it's a complete waste of space,' he would tell me.

'Just keep at it, Chris, she'll probably move on to more

interesting things for you to learn as time moves on. You'll see,' I told him, having not a clue about any of this but trying to give him lots of encouragement.

'All this 'Fuzzbuzz' nonsense that she tries to teach me is driving me nuts. I don't see the point of any of it,' he replied.

Fuzzbuzz is a series of educational books for school age children who experience difficulties with their reading. It is based on phonic and high frequency words and is useful to use with children that need a boost in the basics of education and can improve spelling, which Chris was notoriously poor at in those early days.

As it turned out, his spell of specialised coaching drew to a close in any event as school broke up soon afterwards for the summer holiday break. And, as he was now eleven years old, the new term would herald a move to a different school — he would soon become a 'senior'. And with a new school would come many fresh challenges for him to tackle.

Meanwhile, the years had taken their toll on Judith and myself and we made the decision to separate at around this time. The stressful years with Chris probably hadn't helped too much but there were other factors involved in the break up as I'm sure there are in so many other failing marriages. We knew that there would be a rocky road ahead for the children, but we took the view, rightly or wrongly, that it might be better to make this huge change to their lives now rather than delay it until they became much older.

Chapter 3
A Teenager and bad things emerging

Chris's teenage years kicked off on something of a high note offering us few indications that there might be darker times that loomed ahead. He reached the landmark age of thirteen in March 2001 and two months later Chris, Hannah and myself witnessed a football treat and a brilliant weekend away. Our beloved Blackpool Football Club had reached the Division 2 Play Off Final and we had travelled to the Millennium Stadium in Cardiff to cheer the team on to success — at least, that's what we hoped. The match pitted us against the might of Leyton Orient.

Blackpool did triumph by a margin of four goals to two despite conceding a goal within the first twenty-seven seconds of the match. The club had now won promotion to the third tier of English football. We had a whale of a time in the Welsh capital, along with a multitude of other exultant tangerine-splashed fans. I seem to remember even allowing my children to have a few sips of beer during an evening of long celebration.

Not long after that Hannah and Chris were on my case and clamouring for me to buy them season tickets for the forthcoming season. A wave of football optimism had swept through the town and business was booming at long last at the club's Bloomfield Road headquarters. Our success in South Wales had turned out to be quite an expensive result for me but I didn't care one jot. I would be able to keep a watchful eye on the two of them on Saturday afternoons as they were still only in their early teens.

Chris was excelling with BMX riding and we were all

equally proud that he was now recognised as one of the best and most imaginative riders on the local circuit. I was delighted about his emerging talent and watched him perform as often as I could. I have to admit that watching him was a love—hate kind of relationship for me. It was great to watch him perform but I always feared that he would sustain a nasty injury. He displayed such promise at one stage, that he was actually handed a sponsorship deal from a local trader. His achievements on the ramps inflated his confidence greatly but it was always a double-edged sword for me. He performed at a venue known as Ramp City which was situated in a rural part of Blackpool and I was a regular attendee despite him half frightening me to death many times with his daring stunts. Bunny hops, downside tail-whips, bar spins, pedal grinds and riding nervelessly, at speed up sheer vertical walls were prominent tricks amongst his growing repertoire of tricks.

I considered it vital for him to keep up this all-consuming hobby of his for a number of reasons, not least because it was a positive aid to his hyperactive ways and kept this firmly in check. It was also important to keep his self-confidence perked up after all the bad times he experienced whilst at school — and, sadly, even prior to his schooldays.

I may be forgiven for thinking at the time that life was starting to look brighter for Chris, and by definition, for us all. Perhaps the many trials and tribulations of his early childhood years were starting to ebb away at long last and we could look forward to some much-needed peace and stability in our Lytham home.

The three of us enjoyed the warm summer months together that year, the highlights being short trips away to the Lake district and a week's holiday at the Butlin's holiday camp in Wales. After our arrival at the camp, I recall thinking how much the place had changed for the better since our last visits with my mum, dad and sister back in the late 1960s. Some traditional 'activities' were continuing such as mass cheering in the restaurants when piles of plates had accidentally been dropped and shattered! The chalets were in much better shape too since the old days, although my kids were still less than enamoured even with the greatly improved facilities.

Although life was never easy for us, we were looking forward to the future now with a fair degree of optimism. It would be interesting to see how Chris fared at his new school now that he was a 'senior'. And as he held a Statement of Educational needs would he still be placed in a mainstream class? Do they even have a 'special needs' class at the new school? All would soon be revealed when the autumn school term commenced. Hannah was already at the same school so they would both be learning under the same roof, so to speak.

Once at the high school Chris was placed in a class with everyone else and closely observed. It quickly became apparent that his educational problems were still much in evidence and there had been no improvement since his junior days. His behaviour in class was poor which was likely a direct consequence of his inability to learn like the other pupils. We were pleased, however, to learn that there was a special needs unit based at the school and, as he held a Statement of educational needs, he was invited to learn there from time to time. He attended quite a few times but was less than ecstatic about the whole concept. He felt self-conscious about being in the unit and felt he would be labelled as 'someone thick' by his peers, an expression he often wrongly used to describe himself. It was sad and hurtful as a father to hear one's son talk about himself in this way but we had to soldier on and hope that a solution might be found and better times might conceivably be just around the corner.

It was apparent that Chris had now fallen even further behind at school in terms of his academic progress. He had learned little in the classroom since he was about seven years old and that was now six years ago. As the years had drifted by, the gap in educational development between his class mates and himself had now widened into a chasm. His teachers reported on several occasions, that he was 'off task' in classes and often disruptive which proved a distraction to other pupils. He was even removed from class from time to time because of his erratic conduct. His class friends (and I use the term very loosely) would mercilessly 'take the mickey' out of him because of his educational shortcomings and their cruelness served only to worsen his self-esteem further. This was also evident at home where he was sometimes inclined to be quiet, a little deep and morose. I considered requesting a private meeting with teachers to discuss the best way forward for him but matters would come to a head soon enough anyway.

The end of term 'parents evening' at school, which I had eagerly awaited, turned out to quite an eye opener but for all the wrong reasons. I waited my turn to have the usual discussions with his main teachers and thumbed through examples of his completed work in exercise books and admired a few of his paintings. Although his teachers, quite rightly, attempted to focus on the positive aspects of Chris's overall performance, it quickly dawned on me that the feedback was far from encouraging.

I always maintained that Chris was a much brighter lad than his school grades had ever suggested and, in all likelihood, I felt he did not really warrant 'special needs' support at all. My theory, and it was shared by most of the family, was that his sky-high levels of hyperactivity had long undermined his ability to concentrate and focus on his work properly which resulted in him learning so little. In a nutshell, there was a kind of barrier which prevented him from furthering his education to any real meaningful degree because he was being controlled by his hyperactive condition. We briefly looked at a drug called Ritalin a couple of years before, as previously mentioned, but a few months after the trial, we decided that there was little improvement in his concentration and focus. Ritalin is a medication that can help increase one's ability to pay attention, stay focused on an activity, and control behaviour. We were reminded by doctors that the longer-term effects associated with use of the drug were not fully appreciated then as it was a fairly new medication and more widely used in America at the time.

And so, his 'butterfly mind' was destined to continue fluttering unabated for a considerable while longer. We will return again to the important subject of Chris's Attention Deficit Hyperactivity Disorder again later.

It was at around that time that I was contacted by the headmaster who requested that I called in to have a chat about Chris. This concerned me at first but I said to myself at least we may now be able to get everything out in the open and perhaps find a way forward for him.

At our meeting the subject of Chris's background was discussed at some length and the head also showed interest in his hobbies and interests. He enquired as to how he was faring at home specifically regarding his general behaviour. But other than a few cordialities that was basically it. Was I worrying too much and things were not quite as bad as I imagined? I continued to meet with the head for some while longer and I often sensed that

I was the one who was being placed under the microscope and subjected to some scrutiny. Could I be the major reason for my son's problems? Or was it just plain silly to think this way and maybe I was being just a shade paranoid? As it turned out, the answer to this was the latter. After a few more meetings the two of us chatted freely, sometimes even about neutral topics. I was offered tea and biscuits as the atmosphere in the staff room grew more relaxed.

The conversations between the two of us were never entirely comfortable, however, because I was gradually drip fed a whole catalogue of Chris's misdemeanours whilst in school. One of these, the final one I ever learned about, proved to be the most bitter pill to swallow. Chris had evidently threatened to harm the headmaster in some way as he stood outside his classroom one morning. And it was this unsavoury incident that brought the curtain down on our meetings and an abrupt end. With a single sentence everything had changed dramatically,

'I'm afraid we have reached the end of the road, Mr Frowen,' he told me with a hint of sadness in his voice.

'What exactly do you mean?' I replied.

'We will unfortunately be unable to continue teaching your son at our school and I regret to say that today will be his final day here.'

'Oh heck! Well, what's going to happen now with his schooling?' I said, in something of a daze.

'I will make sure that the education authorities are in contact with you as soon as possible.'

And that effectively was that. My son was permanently excluded from the high school and the decision became operative forthwith. I was completely stunned by the news but when I spoke to Chris about it, he didn't seem overly concerned about this sad turn of events. In fact, I would go further and say he was positively delighted about it all.

'What's going to happen now, Dad?' he asked me as we passed through the school gates for the last time on the way back to the car.

'I'm going to make sure that you don't spend your days idling around playing on your *Nintendo*, that's for sure,' I replied curtly.

'Will I be allowed to go to the trails to practice some new BMX stunts?' The 'trails' was a purpose-built track in Lytham for the benefit of BMX devotees to practice their tricks on.

'I'm okay with that, Chris, but you'll only be allowed on the trails outside school hours,' I affirmed.

'Well, thanks a bunch for that, Dad!' he snarled, with more than a hint of sarcasm.

On the way home, for once in his life, he was subdued and lay slumped in the passenger seat. Meanwhile, a flurry of thoughts whirred uneasily through my mind. Where does this leave Chris's education now as he was still only thirteen years old? What might he get up to now during weekdays if I had to leave him unattended? I couldn't possibly leave him 'home alone' so would I need to find, or employ someone, to care and support him? Worse still, would I be forced into giving up my job to look after him during the week? And worse even than that, how would I then be able to pay my mortgage and all the other bills?

At least it was now a Friday as the news was broken to me and the weekend was upon us. I thought thank heaven for small mercies! I had the buffer of two days get something sorted if I was able to, for the short term at least. My mother had always been my first line of defence with looking after the kids at school holiday times and she had always done a great job but she had, sadly, died a couple of years earlier, at the age of just sixty-eight.

I received lots of support from various friends and family in those difficult early weeks that Chris was at home and the help I received was unbelievable. I was eternally grateful to everyone who had rallied round, even if they could manage only the briefest of stints.

When I first became a single dad back in 1997, I decided to advertise locally to see whether anyone might be interested in opening a single parent club in the area. It was my idea for a local group to become a microcosm of *Gingerbread*, the excellent national charity for single parent families. The response I received was surprisingly good and I was soon able to form a small network of help and support in the area. We held scheduled meetings which gave everyone the opportunity to arrange an occasional 'get together' for themselves, to have a good chat and perhaps let off some steam. The conversations often involved errant ex-partners who were failing to deliver and not coming up to scratch! We shared babysitting duties which enabled hard pressed — and stressed — single mums and dads opportunities to enjoy a welcome night out every now and again. After a few years the group eventually wound down and this was mainly due to members either becoming attached again, remarrying or leaving the area altogether. Many of us did stay in touch with each other afterwards. I happened to be the only single dad in the group out of a total of about fifteen members which I found a little daunting at first!

And so, it was with a fine rallying spirit and oodles of local support that I safely negotiated those challenging first weeks after Chris had left his school. We soon started to receive regular visits from health care workers and education officials and everyone was very keen to find a way for Chris to continue his education. It became apparent that Chris was to be treated as a priority case and the process quickly gathered some pace. Teachers began to call to our house, twice a week for two hours at a time, to give Chris some tuition.

I received a telephone call not long afterwards from an official at the local education authority who asked if I would take Chris along to a school in St Annes on Sea, about four miles away from where we lived. The visit was to determine whether Chris would be a suitable candidate for continuing his school life there. And we needed to establish whether the school would be able to accommodate him with his specific learning issues. The school in question is Red Rose (Dyslexia North West) and a maximum of about forty pupils can be taught there.

As a family, we were never completely convinced that Chris was dyslexic at all and this view has been reinforced by others in the years that followed. Dyslexia is defined as a learning difference which primarily affects reading and writing skills. Dyslexic people may also have difficulty processing and remembering information that they see and hear, which in turn can affect learning and the acquisition of literary skills. It can also impact on other areas such as organisational skills. There are also very positive elements that can be associated with dyslexia. For example, many dyslexic people show strength in areas such as reasoning and in visual and creative ways.

A number of these elements can likely be attributed to Chris but other parts certainly cannot. Chris clearly has huge organisational difficulties but his reading ability is reasonably good and, as in the case of a good wine, this has improved to some degree with age. His skills in processing information are not especially deficient either and he does have an excellent retentive memory. From time to time, he has conjured up some very interesting 'outside the box' type ideas which have often made me think, 'Where on earth did all that come from?' So, all in all, he is a rather mixed bag in terms of dyslexia. I guess that I could describe him as semi-dyslexic, a term which would, I'm sure, sound extremely silly to a psychologist!

Nevertheless, we were thrilled that Chris was accepted at Red Rose and I merrily went out to buy him a new school uniform. Some of the pupils who attended the school had to travel many miles each day from their homes. One of the lads, with whom Chris became very friendly, made the round trip to and from Liverpool each day. And interestingly, very few females appear to be affected by dyslexia. There were seldom more than two girls at the school at any one time while Chris was being taught there.

And so, at thirteen years of age, a new adventure in my son's life was about to begin.

Chris made steady, if unspectacular, progress at Red Rose and was far happier within himself now that he had left his miserable time at the high school well behind him. Each class comprised only six or seven pupils to a teacher. This ratio of pupils to teacher enabled Chris to receive lots of personal attention and the extra support that he needed. He made several friends at the school but unfortunately most of them lived some distance away. It was a pity that he never really had the chance to see too much of them outside of school hours.

There were occasional blips in his performance at the school though. The ADHD factor was very much in evidence as usual and his suspect concentration levels were always lurking in the background. One day, during a toilet break, he successfully managed to worm his way out of a small window in the men's room and proceeded to nonchalantly wander out of school in the direction of the nearby shopping centre. He used this tactic on more than one occasion but, more often than not, he ended up being collared by members of staff who became wise to his ruse and quickly had him returned to the classroom. These minor running away episodes, were maybe the forerunners of his even greater escapes later on.

Chris's school life drew to a close and, in many ways, Red Rose had done him proud. He was a much happier lad now, his self-esteem was probably at its highest level ever and he'd made good friends on the way. He did not take any exams at the school and left there with no qualifications. But he was in pretty good mental and physical shape and looked forward to securing his first proper job. And he was very lucky to land on his feet quickly.

It was only a matter of weeks after his school days were over that Chris was fortunate enough to land himself a plum job. He was employed by a large loft insulation company and I vividly recall driving him to work on that first day. I felt so proud, especially when he waved and smiled meekly at me as he was passing through the gates of his new workplace with a packed lunch box tucked under his arm. He had finally made it in life… or that's what we all thought.

He was tossed in at the deep end, so to speak, and introduced to a gang of other workers whose job it was to travel around the area in a large van to undertake the process of insulating loft areas in houses. They sometimes carried out jobs in commercial premises as well. He arrived home each day enthusing about how he had done this and how he had helped to do that. This was pure music to my ears and I kept everything crossed that the passion for his new venture would run on and on for ever! I was sure that the physical aspect of his job was greatly helping him to burn off his excess energy and was providing some aid to his hyperactive tendencies. He was clearly far more suited to manual working than, for example, clerking in an office. He told me that if he was to work in an office (as I was doing at the time) it would give him constant reminders of his school life and that would be really bad. Those times were 'over and done with for ever', he was always so relieved to point out.

Chris was now becoming a man of means with healthy pay packets rolling in and spending power of his own. I decided that it was high time to introduce him to the world of banking. I chose the same bank for him that I used myself purely for convenience as this would simplify things.

We made an appointment and, once we were inside the bank, Chris was bamboozled with the plethora of paperwork he was asked to sign and with the questions that flew at him.

'What limit would you like to set me to for your overdraft, Mr Frowen?'

'Would you agree to go paperless with your bank statements?'

'How about opening up an investment account as well? We can offer you some very good interest rates at the moment?'

To underline his complete, but perfectly understandable lack of knowledge of the banking system, as we were leaving the bank his parting shot to the official who dealt with us was, 'Just one more thing, please. When do I get all the money then?'

The bank official and myself shared wry glances but Chris was deadly serious and couldn't understand what all our mirth was about.

'Um, let's take one thing at a time, just for now,' the bank official replied to Mr Frowen junior with a reassuring smile.

Chris was totally bemused by his first experience in the big, wide world of banking. He proudly clutched a whole pile of paperwork in his arms which included a brand-new paying in book. The latter item was to become the cause of a significant amount of bother for me before long. So the salaries from his new employers would soon be credited to his freshly opened account and Chris gleefully awaited the money to arrive. He was well on his way now.

Everything continued to run smoothly at work for quite a while and his new bank account was in tip-top shape too. In fact, each time he viewed his bank statement he was over the moon as he gazed in wonderment at the healthy, and rising, balances. There was, however, an extra factor involved with his sudden large influx of cash, which he was blithely unaware of. When I eventually discovered one of the reasons why Chris had suddenly become so flush with cash, I was not best pleased at all!

He was now a man of some means and I was over the moon when he decided to invite me to dine with him one evening at a posh, local steak restaurant — and all at his expense. Well, this is definitely a 'first', I mused and accepted his offer without a second thought. And long may generous offers like this one continue, I thought.

One of Chris's major problems, which persist through to the present day, is his inability to hang on to money for any meaningful length of time. He has never really understood the meaning of words such as 'budgeting' and 'save' despite my many attempts to coach him in this area. Nevertheless, our meal was extremely enjoyable and I was treated to the 'whole Monty'. And to reinforce what I have said, as we were leaving the restaurant, he handed the delighted waiter a ten-pound note, which was a jolly decent tip at the time!

My son's 'spend, spend, spend' mentality, a phrase

popularised in the 1960s by a lucky young lady who had won mega bucks on the football pools, continued as he marvelled at the size of the salary he was receiving, from these wonderful loft insulation people. Expensive items of designer clothing flooded into the house with alarming regularity along with several top of the range aftershaves. I have to admit that it did seem to be an inordinately attractive wage for a sixteen-year-old but I decided to let it be for the time being.

By chance, a statement for my own bank account popped through the letterbox around the same time and, after some scrutiny, I was puzzled to note that my credit balance was far less healthy than it ought to have been. I decided to pay my branch a visit to query this and, armed with the statement and my cheque book, I went along straight away. I told the clerk that I very often deposited cheques with them and even a cursory scan of my statement revealed that all these entries were missing. Fortunately, I managed to stay calm and non-confrontational during our discussion because it soon became evident that the whole mix up was entirely my own fault.

It became evident that I had inadvertently been using Chris's paying-in book to deposit my own cheques. This error had gradually compounded itself as the same error occurred over and over again for several weeks. Hundreds and hundreds of pounds worth of *my own* cheques were being added to my son's account!

The bank clerk and myself attempted to laugh it off but it really wasn't all that funny. In the final reckoning, there was nothing that could be done to rectify my howling blunders and to reimburse me, because I had only myself to blame. The upshot of this, of course, was that I was seriously out of pocket but I made absolutely sure that the same situation never arose again by keeping our respective paying in books completely separate and well under control. And to this very day, Chris remains totally unaware of the episode. But I'm certain that he soon noticed significant changes to his burgeoning income stream.

The epitaph to this episode might be mildly humorous I suppose, now that it's long over and done with. It didn't take me long to work out that the beautiful steak meal that Chris had kindly treated me to was actually paid for by me!

After a few weeks assisting in the process of insulating loft spaces, Chris was handed the chance to undertake the more interesting role of cavity wall insulation. We saw this as evidence that he was making some real progress and were so pleased that he seemed to be enjoying, and thriving even, in his fledgling working life. His promotion to cavity wall work turned out eventually to be the genesis of adolescent problems and ultimately led to a slow decline into a downward spiral.

His new role demanded that he travelled further afield to take on his cavity wall jobs and the excursions took him to places as far away as Manchester and Liverpool. He found himself crammed in the back of a van for hours on end with several other guys who made up the rest of his work gang. It became apparent that some of the other chaps smoked 'wacky backy' on the way to help alleviate boredom during tedious journeys in the van. It wasn't long before Chris had to sample some himself as he didn't want to appear the odd one out and wanted to please his peers. The effects of these joints soon saw him giggling and getting 'high' along with all the rest of them. His new found interest certainly made the long trips away more palatable and, in all fairness, he always told me everything he got up to when he returned home, whether the news was good or bad. This phase of smoking dodgy stuff continued for some while and, although I knew all about it, I didn't observe any real change to his health, moods or demeanour… for a while at least. And I wasn't overly concerned because it seemed that no harm was actually being caused and, as Chris would tell me himself, 'everyone does it these days, Dad'.

For the uninitiated, and I definitely included myself in that category, especially in the early days of this phase, the 'wacky baccy' term is a drugs slang for cannabis or marijuana. The full extent of my own experiences with illegal substances was limited to my tuning in to rock bands such as *The Doors* in my teenage years as they, lyrically, always seemed to be getting 'higher and higher'. I also learned very quickly that one can detect the scent of the stuff, a strong and unmistakeable musky odour, from quite a distance away.

I discovered through accessing the internet that cannabis contains more than one hundred active ingredients, or cannabinoids. Some cannabinoids can have euphoric or psychoactive effects. By this stage I was starting to become more than a little concerned, not only because of what I had read in books and on the internet, but also because Chris was beginning to develop mood swings and seemed prone to spells of irritability and snappiness for no apparent reason. It was also noticeable that he was staying in his room for long stretches of time but I hoped that this change in behaviour could merely be a normal teenage thing. His sister Hannah was equally concerned about Chris. She thought that his job, albeit profitable and very financially rewarding, was causing him far more harm than good because of negative influences that his peers were having on him.

A few weeks later, Chris's first sortie in the workplace unfortunately came to a sudden end. His employers were forced into making staff cuts and it was a case of 'last in, first out'. And Chris had definitely been one of the last ones in. The damage caused by drug smoking was already evident as he was now well into the habit. He struggled after that to find another job despite my taking him along to the local job centre several times each week. So now, bored and fed up, he tended to console himself smoking joints and idling around the house and aimlessly wiling the time away with friends.

It was a serious dilemma time for me. He had made a good number of local friends over the years, and it seemed to me that the majority of them were also habitual 'weed' users. They started to use our summerhouse in the rear garden as a main venue for their evening activities.

He was now nearly eighteen years old, sturdy and about six feet in height. Up to then, I was always able to tell Chris what to do or where we were going to today. Signs were appearing that it was fast becoming a case of should I *ask* him whether he would do this or would he please do that for me!

I agreed to allow Chris and his mates to spend evenings in the summerhouse after some deep soul searching. My logic told me that had I refused them the use of my garden haven and sent them packing elsewhere they would only have moved to another joint and got up to exactly the same antics. At home, I would at least be able to keep a firm eye on what was going on and it would also lessen the risk of alienating Chris and keep him 'on side' with me. Much to my relief, this unpleasant phase soon faded away, as did the acrid stench of weed which seemed to find its way into every nook and cranny. The fickleness of teenagers' pursuits had done me proud, just this once.

The subject of substance issues reared its ugly head again a month or two later when Chris, now into his nineteenth year, acquired a stash of what appeared to look like a cocaine-like white substance. I was busily tidying up his bedroom one

Saturday while he was out riding around on his BMX when I made a shocking discovery. As I made his bed and bashed his pillow into some shape, I felt something fairly solid beneath. Lifting the pillow gently I found to my horror a large sized plastic bag jam-packed full of a suspicious-looking white powder. My first thoughts followed the lines of, 'Oh my God, it's cocaine and there's got to be literally thousands of pounds worth of the stuff here. Where the Hell, has he got it from? I've gotta get it out of my house right now!'

It was now late morning and I thought long and hard about the best thing I could do about this and how exactly I should tackle Chris about it. My thought processes ranged from the rational to downright irrational. Should I take the bag immediately to the police and report to them where I had found it? But then I thought if I was to pick up the bag it would have my fingerprints on it and I might become implicated in some way. Should I ring members of my family and see what they think? Maybe I should bury the bag somewhere and forget that the whole matter had ever happened? And my final thought was, should I flush the whole lot down the sink and have done with it?

I dismissed the last option almost straight away. My reasoning was that if Chris was temporarily storing the stuff for someone and it simply vanished from the face of the earth then he could find himself in almighty trouble. I had clearly been watching far too many television crime dramas!

I eventually decided that the safest thing to do was to bury it somewhere, at least for the time being, until I had formed a clearer plan. And I had to take careful note of exactly where its resting place would be. I decided to bury it deep in a flower border in my back garden. I then cleaned myself up and awaited uneasily for further developments once Chris returned from his bike ride.

I paced anxiously backwards and forwards across the lounge for seemingly an eternity and peered endlessly from my front window waiting for a BMX bike to appear. I tackled him head on the moment he walked through the door.

'Hi, Chris, had a good ride on your bike then? What's that bag of white stuff that I've found under your pillow this morning?' I asked him in a matter-of-fact fashion.

'Oh. that. It's something I ordered on the internet and it arrived in the post yesterday. It's come from China, I think,' he replied, equally matter of fact.

'Well, what the Hell is it?' I bawled.

'It's called BZP. Don't worry, Dad, it's one hundred percent legal and it only cost me about thirty quid for the lot. I've done really well, don't you think?' he answered, sounding very pleased with himself.

'Well, it's panicked me half to death, Chris. And anyway, I've buried it now'.

'You'd better not have done, Dad. You've no right to touch my stuff.'

I reckoned that I had *every* right to 'touch his stuff' as it was in my house. A long discussion followed which gradually made a number of things much clearer. The substance was evidently a so-called 'legal high' and was openly on sale across Britain at the time, and over the internet too. This drug, and others like it, are typically man-made chemical substances designed to act as banned drugs. He told me that it was very popular on the club scene and that people used it as an amphetamine.

What he had told me was all fine and dandy but the damned stuff was still buried in my garden and I told him that it would be highly preferable if it was not allowed to contaminate my prized blooms any longer.

The episode was quickly brought to a conclusion when I handed Chris £30 in cash as reimbursement for his stash, an action which was seriously contrary to my better judgement but it did bring about a swift resolution. All that now remained was to dig up the bag and flush the whole lot down the sink in front of an aghast Chris. The only strict condition to the deal I struck with him was that I never wanted to see any more of that, or any similar stuff, anywhere near my house again. And I also insisted on no more suspect internet deals.

The synthetic BZP drug was outlawed a short while afterwards and became illegal and, thank goodness, was no longer available over the internet either.

Chris had now reached nineteen years of age and he found a job locally in the welding trade. He seemed to enjoy his time working for a wrought iron gate company and I kept everything crossed that this might signal a turning point at the tail end of his teenage years, and allow him the chance to go completely straight. I was pleased to learn that he took to the welding trade really well and his bosses expressed satisfaction that he was applying himself solidly to his tasks. But once again, after a couple of months he was shown the door through no fault of his own at all. He was surplus to their current requirements as trade had recently dropped off quite substantially. I felt so terribly sorry for him because he felt badly let down and it was very possible that he might have made a good, solid career from welding. And this brief flirtation in the welding trade, at nineteen years of age, remains to this day, Chris's last ever paid job.

In the space of a few months shortly before Chris left his teen years behind him, two events took place which in their own ways affected him quite badly — one in an emotional sense and the other in a physical way.

Our family cat, who went by the name of 'Cable' (more about his choice of name later), disappeared one night and failed to return home. He was about ten years old, as near as we could tell, because we had adopted him some years earlier and never learned his full history. Chris loved Cable to bits. He was completely black in colour other than a few flecks of white near his chest, but it seemed that he had not been too lucky this time. The three of us produced posters and distributed them around the area and handed them to anyone who we felt could help to find him. We also posted a few in shop windows. Three days later our public appeal produced a result, but it was hardly the one that we had hoped for.

A neighbour, who lived several doors away, called at our house in response to the poster and told us sorrowfully that, a few days earlier, he had spotted a cat lying down in his back garden. He discovered, on closer examination, that it appeared to have died in its sleep. The elderly gentleman had no clue as to the cat's owners so he decided to bury him, respectfully, beneath the tree where he had found him. On hearing the awful news, Chris immediately hurried to find a spade and then made a beeline for the man's house. He came home ten minutes later in tears, cradling a soil-coated Cable in his arms.

We quickly warned Chris that what he was doing could easily represent a health hazard but he insisted on holding Cable tight for a good while longer. We reburied our beloved pussy cat in our garden and Chris bought a small concrete statue of a cat which we erected as a memorial. He later told me that no other cat would ever be able to compare to Cable. That was until a new moggie, Dinky, appeared on the scene a little while later.

The origins of the name 'Cable' date back to when I was the holder of the dubious title of Blackpool Football Club's official mascot in the 1990s. The mascot just happened to be known as 'Cable Cat', named after the telecommunications company who were the club's shirt sponsors. For some reason, my kids were kind of proud that their dad once used to prance around on a football field and got up to all sorts of allegedly entertaining antics!

Matters were made worse still when, a few weeks post-Cable, Chris suffered a nasty BMX riding accident at Ramp City when he attempted a particularly difficult dare-devil, Evel Knievel-style trick.

I was present when the accident occurred and I rushed a clearly shocked Chris to the local Accident and Emergency unit at the hospital where he had been born some years earlier. He had fallen heavily and awkwardly on his right arm and from a great height, breaking both the ulna and radius bones in his left forearm but his injuries could have been a whole lot worse. He found himself in plaster and was effectively house-bound for a good while after that. The accident put paid to any further BMX aspirations for a very long time.

Whether the two disparate events had any longer-term detrimental effects on Chris's well-being the following year we will never know but it has often given me plenty of food for thought.

So he celebrated his twentieth birthday on 20 March as a special party with a large gathering of family and friends was organised. While everyone was getting high (on alcohol only, I might add) and having plenty of fun I couldn't help but allow my mind to wander for a short while. I imagined the joys, or otherwise, that the years in my son's twenties might have in store for him. Ever the optimist, I thought that whatever happens we can work things out together.

Chapter 4
21ˢᵗ Birthday Misery and the 'Great Escape'

By the time Chris turned twenty years of age he was really beginning to struggle. He was failing to pay due attention to many situations, his concentration levels were poor and his behaviour was increasingly unpredictable and even chaotic. It was evident that his ADHD condition was continuing into his adulthood. Experts in the field have suggested that approximately two thirds of all children who suffer from ADHD discover that it gradually fades away once they become adults. Chris is a tiny part of that unlucky one third. ADHD is a group of behavioural symptoms that includes inattentiveness, hyperactivity and impulsiveness. It was the impulsivity factor which probably impacted him most detrimentally as Chris reached adulthood and progressed into his twenties.

Since he'd had the misfortune to lose his welding job two months previously, his moods had been low and he had entered a depressive phase. This was due in part to his increased alcohol intake, which was becoming more noticeable. He often enjoyed a few pints a night during his teenage years but it had been mainly a social thing then amongst friends. He was bought a bottle of whiskey for Christmas by a relative and seemed to immediately acquire a taste for it. He had done all the usual stuff that lads of his age did such as drinking in pubs with his mates and then moving on to night clubs when the mood took him. And being a good-looking young man, he had little difficulty attracting the ladies. He took delight in introducing his new partners to me and

I kept my fingers crossed that he was maturing into a fine and well-adjusted young man. Alas, very few of his female relationships seemed to last for too long. This saddened me because I was sure that a good lady in his life would have given him some welcome stability and could have been 'the making of him'. But there's bound to be someone out there who will make you happy and vice versa, I would repeatedly say to him. All these social activities were normal fare, I guess, for a youth who was discovering new things all the time and navigating a way through the maze of his first flush of manhood.

So it was clear that he now preferred to drink spirits, which I felt was acceptable as long as it was kept under some control. He frequently told me at the time that having a few drinks was a form of escapism for him to help achieve temporary solace from 'my crap life', as he was often inclined to express it.

I encouraged him to go out more and to re-establish contact with his friends and to socialise more. The two of us did quite a lot together which at least got him out of the house now and again. We enjoyed rounds of golf together on local courses and he loved the sport so much that I bought him a set of left-handed clubs. Chris and I are both naturally left-handed; I play golf badly but the 'right-handed' way and Chris has an ugly-looking wrong way round swing! It may look pretty bad to an educated golfer's eye but I have to say that when he manages to 'middle' the ball with his metal driver he can send the ball flying for miles!

We maintained our passion for football, and went to matches both home and away in support of our local team. One or two full away-day trips hold particularly happy memories for us. He was very well behaved when we went on days away from home and especially when football was on his menu — this was more than likely due to the fact that his mind was fully occupied.

Blackpool Football Club, by this time, had risen to the dizzy heights of the second tier of the English football league. The team was beginning to look a decent bet for a shot at promotion to the promised land of the Premier League in the not-too-distant future. The improved quality of football, allied to the air of optimism that circulated around the town, resulted in an increase in attendances and a better atmosphere which gave us all a real buzz. I still have Chris's Blackpool shirt in my wardrobe with 'Frowen' and the number '17' imprinted on the back. Sadly, he hasn't had too many chances to wear it in recent years because of hospitalisation but it's here for him when he is able to return to the fold. I have never discovered the reason why he chose that particular number for his shirt — after all, seventeen was neither his or any of his family's birthdays, nor his age, the shirt number of his favourite player or anything else of notable significance. But I suppose that was just pure Chris — always so full of unique and quirky ways.

He was probably sick to the back teeth of me pecking at him, giving him advice about how to make a success of his life and how to use his time more usefully but I meant well and it was always said in his best interests. My gentle coaxing, however, did tend to fall on stony ears as he continued to booze and smoke the dreaded weed as often as his now-limited funds would allow him to.

We occasionally went on day trips into the Lancashire countryside and, to my delight, he thoroughly enjoyed our strolls out in the wilds. He told me that he loved to get away from everything every now and again and to do 'normal things' with me. He always had a fair nucleus of friends but saw very little of them and spent much of his time alone. This in itself did precious little to boost the state of his mental health and well-being.

One day we decided to go a hike in the country and our route took us to rural Garstang, which is about twenty miles from our home. We went for a pleasant five mile walk which took us through many fields, over the M6 motorway (via a bridge), and well beyond. Presently, we headed back and eventually we wandered into the quaint little historic town feeling somewhat tired and thirsty and ready for a decent lunch. As we hunted around for a suitable pub in which to eat, we mooched idly around when I suddenly realised that I was chattering on to myself. Chris had vanished into thin air! I bobbed my head into a few shops we had passed to check whether he had wandered in without telling me which is always a distinct possibility where Chris is concerned. But there was not a trace of him anywhere. I resorted to hollering out his name around the streets but this was not successful either.

My raised voice seemed to attract the attention of several passers-by who wandered over to check the reason for my concern. They learned that I had mislaid my lad and were keen to help me look for him. I thanked them for their help but, in my haste, I omitted to mention that he was not a toddler! They fired lots of questions at me that people normally ask when someone has become lost. One after the other the questions flooded in and I scarcely had an opportunity to respond or to explain the situation more clearly,

'Can you remember what is he wearing?'

'What colour is his hair? Is it long or short?'

'Has he ever done this kind of thing in the past?'

'Does he know someone who lives close by who he may have called on?'

My four helpers soon swelled to about ten and they proceeded to parade around the narrow, cobbled streets calling out Chris's name and quizzing shoppers. But he remained AWOL although of a completely different nature to the type we had become traditionally accustomed to. An elderly lady became a little tearful as she stressed that we must report it to the local police straight away. The area was agog with a gaggle of Good Samaritans who all did their level best to locate Chris. One chap, with a large dog in tow, placed his arm on my shoulder and told me not to worry because 'they always show up eventually'. I winced because I knew that he was barking up the wrong tree (no pun intended).

Finally, Chris did show up, as I fully expected he would. He was smiling and cradling a half empty can of beer in his hand — all twenty years of age, resplendent with designer stubble and a full six feet in height. My helpers were agape and stood motionless. I will never forget their bemused expressions as I gave Chris a good ticking off and told him never to wander off and leave me again!

I was just about managing to cope with Chris's worsening behaviour as Christmas 2008 was approaching. I always tried to keep my emotions well in check and not to allow my guard to slip. I found that this has been the best way to keep my head well above the water line and to maintain some normality. As I have mentioned earlier, I do largely tend to look on the bright side of life and, with another new year fast appearing on the horizon, I said to my son optimistically, 'Come on, Chris. Let's make 2009 your big breakthrough year.'

'Yeah, right, Dad,' he replied blankly, not really having a clue what I was on about.

Despite his disinterest in my attempt to inspire him, l carried on regardless of the obstacles I would likely be facing in the coming year. This optimistic outlook on life can sometimes come unstuck and events that began to unfold early in the new year proved this point perfectly.

As the new year dawned it heralded the start of a horrible phase for Chris. A sinister new development had come into Chris's life which was the major cause of a marked decline in his mental health and ultimately lead to his first spell in hospital two months later. The months of January and February were cold and miserable enough anyway but Chris's rapidly worsening health made it appear like a 'double whammy'. It was difficult to be positive about virtually anything as everything changed for the worse. Even in the office, my standard of work slipped considerably. My bosses had a pretty good understanding of the pressure I was under in my home life and it was gratifying that they were supportive. My work colleagues were also aware of the situation at home and knew that flare ups could occur at any time.

Chris's mental health was now in rapid decline and we had no idea how to halt the roller coaster that was speeding downhill and almost out of control. He was in uncharted territory as far as mental health was concerned and it was such a worrying time for us. And a single, nasty word was responsible for all the chaos and bedlam and that was 'skunk'.

To weed connoisseurs, skunk can be described simply as premium strength cannabis. Cannabis itself has often been dismissed as a relatively harmless street drug, especially when compared to class 'A' drugs such as cocaine and heroin. Skunk is linked to brain changes and can make some users feel confused, anxious or paranoid and hallucinations can occur. When Chris was introduced to this unpleasant stuff it proved to be a tipping point. He had always been vulnerable to dodgy illegal substances but this was quite different and proved to be very damaging. Once he started smoking this super-weed his moods swung about wildly. And his mental health plummeted to further depths.

Early in the new year I had made provisional plans to mark Chris's twenty first birthday and a few surprises were in store for him. The big day would take place on 20 March but as things began to unravel, I had little drive, inclination or even the heart to organise anything that we could 'set in stone'. I feared and prepared for the worst — although I naturally always hoped for the best, my natural optimism was tested severely, to well beyond its upper limit. In my wildest dreams, I never imagined that my son could be locked up for in hospital under Section 3 of the Mental Health Act on his twenty first birthday. But this outcome was looking more and more likely with each day that passed.

I learned that Chris had made the dubious 'progression' to skunk purely by accident. He had done some kind of deal with a mate, whose name remains unknown, and he managed to obtain a bagful of this stuff. He had become more secretive by this time and was telling me less and less about what he was getting up to and about his 'extra-curricular' activities. I never did discover the specifics of his unsavoury skunk deal but it could have involved an excellent quality mobile phone which Chris acquired from somewhere. I noticed he was accumulating quite a collection of mobiles but considered that it would not be the right time to quiz him about this. To be honest, I didn't care one jot about how the deal had been conducted or what it had exactly involved — all that mattered was that it had happened. And the result of smoking the stuff was both swift and devastating for him.

One evening, Chris decided to share his new stash with some mates and they collectively 'enjoyed' a beanfeast of a time by all accounts. It was purely rank bad luck for Chris that illegal substances always had a bad effect on him although they seemed to have a less detrimental impact on his mates.

The skunk made Chris feel confused and anxious. Paranoia was also in evidence, which I had never witnessed before in him, and it was a scary development. He was even having hallucinations at one point.

I know that it may have been illogical to have these thoughts but I often felt a sense of guilt about all the bad things that were happening to Chris, and had happened in his life. I helped to bring him into this world with the usual parental hopes, dreams and ambitions for him. We naturally wanted him to enjoy and savour all the adventures that life held in store for him. But there had not been too much fun in his life and I could get no further than to point a finger firmly at myself for his problems. I wondered whether his mental health issues could have, at least in part, a genetic root as I soul-searched for answers. I carried out extensive online research, and managed to trace my own family tree back several generations to hunt for clues that might help me to understand more about Chris. The venture did not bear much fruit but I did learn one or two inconsequential nuggets of information on the way, such as the fact that it appeared my paternal great grandfather had suffered from very poor vision and I have clearly inherited his mild affliction! I wondered whether the break-up of his mum and dad's marriage, when he was only eight years old, was an important contributory factor. Or maybe, just maybe, I could have done much more during his upbringing to give him the best possible start in life.

I will never know the answers to the purely hypothetical questions that I wrestled with for some while but I knew one thing for certain. I pledged to do my utmost to get him back on life's correct path no matter what it entailed. I know this might sound a little gruesome to some people but I would crawl through a tunnel of broken glass to help Chris if he was ever in trouble or danger. I probably wouldn't be in such wonderful shape as I reached the end of that tunnel but I would always endeavour to do my best, all the same!

It was now the middle of March and Chris was sinking deeper into a psychotic state and we were just a week away from his birthday. Chris's mum and myself were now in daily contact, comparing notes about his worsening health and trying to fathom the best way to improve things, if that was at all possible. On 14 March, she decided to take Chris to Blackpool Victoria Hospital because of concerns about his increasing symptoms of depression, thoughts of suicide, paranoid ideas and the belief that he was hearing voices in his head. As a result of this hospital visit with his mum, it was decided that Chris would be assessed, as a matter of some urgency, by the local Crisis Team.

Indeed, the situation was so pressing that it was as soon as the next day that Chris was taken to Accident and Emergency under Section 136 and detained under Section 2 of the Mental Health Act. By way of some explanation, Section 136 allows someone ill or vulnerable to be taken to a place of safety, for example if a police officer is concerned one could well have a mental disorder and should be seen as soon as possible by a mental health professional. And Section 2 of the Mental Health Act provides for someone to be detained in hospital for a period of up to 28 days under a legal framework for an assessment and treatment of their mental disorder. A 'Section 2' is very often graded upwards to a Section 3 if a condition does not improve. Chris's conversion to a Section 3 did take place eventually but not until about a month later which is often the case.

So, five days before his birthday, he was put on an acute level mental health ward at Parkwood hospital, Blackpool, and kept under close observation. I visited him a day after his arrival there and he was in an awful state. I was greeted by a heart-rending scene as he looked so sad, bewildered and bedraggled.

It was only a matter of a week later that he was already looking so much better. I was amazed that such a huge transformation could have happened in such a short period of time. His newly prescribed medications had clearly kicked in and they were having a remarkable impact.

His improvement was so encouraging that the ward staff decided to give him an early taste of leave within the hospital grounds together with an escort to accompany him. The result of this first spell of leave proved to be absolutely disastrous. He managed to 'escape' from his escort after scrambling up an enormously steep wall and disappeared on the other side and away into the ether. His absconding career was set to continue unabated for the next ten years and had now officially kicked off.

His first escape episode was far and away the most harrowing and worrying experience that we ever encountered. And the incident, to this day, remains the worst of all his thirty or so successful escapes for several reasons. It was the first time that he had absconded and with that factor alone came the great unknown. We were completely in the dark about the whole situation and in a state of some panic. What would happen next? I vividly recollect how unconcerned the ward staff seemed to be at the time. This is perfectly understandable, of course, because they are trained to deal with these kinds of incidents all the time and have to remain calm for everyone's sake. We feared the worst and were left to hope for the best outcome and a rapid recapture and his return to the ward. The main reason why this first absconding event was so tortuous is because in the final reckoning he managed to stay free and 'at large' in the community for three whole days!

We were unable to come up with any ideas as to where Chris might have been heading for or what his intentions could be, that is if he had any at all. He had spoken to me about suicide once or twice around that time and I tried hard not to think that he might be on a mission to harm himself — or even worse. I later concluded that his most likely plan would probably be to find his way home to Lytham to see Hannah and myself but mainly to see his cat! He worships Dinky, and always misses him enormously when he's out of commission in hospital. And to the present day, whenever we speak on the phone or during my visits, the first question he nearly always asks is, 'How's Dinky pussy cat and is he coping all right without me?'

The long hike from Parkwood hospital, which is situated to the east of the Blackpool town centre, to our home in Lytham was ten or eleven miles but I knew that Chris would be able to make it, maybe with the help of a few pit stops, along the way. It started to look like my prediction would come true after I received mobile calls from two of his friends who had seen and spoken to him as he foot slogged south in the general direction of Lytham. They expressed concern about his odd demeanour and commented that he seemed distant and confused. I could virtually track his exact route on a local map because of the help I was receiving but decided not to get in my car and drive around the streets to try and intercept him. Meanwhile, the police had contacted me for additional information about Chris. They were especially interested in his current state of mental health and quizzed me as to whether he might be able to cause serious harm to himself or to others. I couldn't be positive about this, especially given the events of the last few hours, but I asked the police to work on the assumption that he could easily be dangerous to everyone, including himself.

The police paid me a personal visit at home. I was worried out of my wits but the two officers were excellent at keeping me calm and reasonably relaxed. They said, reassuringly, they were sure he would be picked up before long and returned to hospital and added that this sort of thing happens quite regularly so I wasn't to worry too much. If my recollections are correct, they quoted some encouraging statistics which revealed that in an overwhelming majority of similar cases there are good outcomes. This gave me a lot of comfort but I still couldn't help thinking about the other few percent that have unfortunate endings.

Chris had apparently 'escaped' from Parkwood Hospital at around lunchtime and the light was failing, as we were still in March and the days were short. Little did I know then that this unfolding drama was set to continue for another two full days.

Judith was on the phone to me very regularly. I asked her whether she would like to come to our house and join Hannah and me for what could turn out to be an all-night vigil. She decided to stay put, preferring instead to be kept informed of developments by telephone. We were both anxious but I tried to appear positive about the situation. Judith said to me, 'Do you think he's all right, Rob? Anything could've happened to him by now. It's just so worrying, I'm scared stiff.'

'Try not to worry, Judith. I know that's very easy for me to say. He'll be found soon safe and well and be back in hospital before you know it. I feel sure that he'll be just fine,' I replied calmly but I'm sure I was just as anxious.

'Why are you always so irritatingly optimistic?' she added wryly.

'I dunno. I guess I'm just stuck with it!'

As the 'nearest relative' I would more than likely be the first port of call from the police if there were any new developments.

The term 'nearest relative', incidentally, refers to a family member who has certain responsibilities and powers if one is detained in hospital under the Mental Health Act. These include the right to information and to discharge in certain situations.

Meanwhile. Hannah told me that she somehow sensed that her brother was by now quite close to us in Lytham. She decided to act on her hunch and spent most of the evening wandering around the darkened streets, deserted parks and late-night shops of the town. But all her efforts all came to nothing. There was no sign of Chris anywhere and, to make matters a little worse still, he had effectively become incommunicado because he had either switched off his mobile phone or it had run out of battery.

It was late March and the night was damp and cold. I slept fitfully and uneasily on the settee, always ready for a knock on the door or a phone call that I knew might never come. I awoke very early, still feeling tired, but my first thought was to wonder whether Chris had actually managed to get any sleep at all, wherever he was. So we were into day two of the drama and were no further forward.

I received an early morning visit from two police officers. They enquired as to whether I had heard anything from Chris or from anyone who may have sighted him. I said that I hadn't heard a thing at all and asked them the same question. I had probably posed a purely rhetorical question because I felt I already knew the answer. I could not imagine that Chris would ever voluntarily contact the police or enter one of their stations unless he was in absolutely desperate straits. It would be a 'no go' area for him because, for some obscure reason, he seemed to harbour a rather unhealthy regard for the police force in general at that time. The police officers assured me that they would be redoubling their efforts to find him safe and handed me their own phone numbers and urged me to contact them if there were any new leads that they could follow up.

And that, basically, was that. Nothing else happened for the remainder of the morning and we now felt more dismal than ever. Soon after our lunch, (although I seem to recall that I ate virtually nothing) I decided to have a cycle ride around Lytham in an attempt to burn off some nervous tension that had built up in me. And I said to Hannah as I left home, 'Who knows, Hannah — I might even see Chris while I'm out on my travels.'

And incredibly, that is exactly what happened.

As I cycled along Henry Street, a small road in the Lytham town centre, on my way to the Promenade I instantly spotted Chris's distinctive, loping gait as he marched along the pavement directly across the road from me. I shouted out his name and he instantly swung his head around and saw me. He seemed unsure as to whether he should run away or come across to see me. Instead, he stood rooted to the spot as I scooted my bike over to meet him. It was now the twenty third of March, three days after his twenty first birthday, and my mind was all over the place and pretty scrambled at the time. So I said my something to him that was probably quite banal.

'Hello, Chris, I've got you something really nice for your birthday. Would you like me to bring it to you? I'll go home and get it for you if you'd like to stay here and wait for me.'

His blank expression told me that he was in a world of his own and away with the fairies. It made me instantly think — what on earth did he get up to last night? There was no way that I could have possibly predicted what his next move would have been. As I dismounted from my bike, he pushed me over very roughly and I fell clumsily and heavily into the road. He unceremoniously dragged the bike from under me and shot off with it, without saying a single word. He pedalled away into the distance and probably out of sight. I use the word 'probably' because I was still lying prostrate on the ground and unable to see very much at all, save the tarmac beneath me. A few shoppers hurried over to check what had happened as I was spread-eagled in the road. My first thought was to check if I was hurting anywhere but a brief examination revealed that I was reasonably uninjured. In the shock of the moment, I muttered something quite silly to the folk who looked over at me: 'It's all right, he's just my son. It's nothing to worry about, he's often like this.'

One by one, they wandered away from me, mystified by it all. I was still in a state shock but gradually gathered my thoughts. I felt so relieved that Chris was still very much in the land of the living. I limped slowly home, minus my bike, and pondered my next move as I struggled back. Hannah was waiting at the door to greet me. I had texted her to tell her that I had a sighting of Chris which would pacify her a little. I omitted to tell her the less savoury parts of the incident. On my arrival home, even before I'd attended to a throbbing hip, I rang one of the police officers who'd visited earlier, to update him on what had just happened. At least we knew that he was somewhere in the vicinity — or at least, he *was* in the locale up until about an hour ago. I really wished I hadn't bought a new bike weeks earlier, because I formed the distinct impression that I was unlikely to ever see it again.

I knew that Chris was well 'out of it' and could not possibly have been thinking straight when he unceremoniously bundled me off my bike. He had never attempted to harm me before in any way — or since that day, for that matter. I prayed and hoped that the police, now armed with this important update, would swamp the town with officers, locate him, and return him safely to his ward in Blackpool.

His freedom continued throughout the rest of the day and into another evening. It was at about 11pm as I was settling down to another night on the settee that I noticed a strange whirring noise outside. I ventured out and saw that it was a helicopter flying overhead. It transpired that the 'chopper squad' had been called out to assist in the hunt for Chris. I learned a while later that the cost of launching a police helicopter and circling the area for an hour was not a cheap operation by any stretch of the imagination and I was eternally grateful for their efforts. But their costly operation was to yield no fruit either. When this whole episode was well and truly over, weeks later, I quizzed Chris during a very informal debrief, as to how he managed to evade the attention of the police helicopter while it had hovered overhead. I was amazed and, oddly, felt a little proud when he told me that he had hidden the whole time under a large sheet of corrugated iron. He was well aware that there would be heat-searching equipment on board and that he would be completely undetectable while he remained concealed underneath.

I finally managed to nod off some time after midnight and sank slowly into another restless, haunted sleep and again on my settee.

I was awakened in the small hours by a strange, delicate sensation of someone kissing me gently on the cheek and could hear a curious, quiet whispering. I thought I must still be dreaming. Another whispering sound followed, a little louder this time, and my eyes flickered open. There was Chris standing right in front of me in my lounge and smiling at me like a Cheshire cat! I came rapidly to my senses and smiled back, taking good care not to spook him which might cause him to run off again. I recall saying something to him quietly along the broad lines of,

'Oh, hello, Chris, how are you? I've been so worried and wondered where you've been all this time. How did you manage to get in here, by the way?'

'It was dead easy, Dad, you should be more careful about your security!'

It seemed that I had accidentally left the patio doors unlocked and he had easily managed to come inside. He told me that he had to undertake a lot of 'garden hopping' to eventually work his way into our back garden.

He was so contrite and apologetic about the incident in Lytham centre and asked me if I had been hurt. I told him that, luckily, I felt fine while I sneakily hid away a bottle of paracetamol capsules that were by my side. My damaged hip was still quite sore.

'Don't worry about me, Chris, I'll live!' I said to him.

His mood was in complete contrast to his horridness the previous afternoon. He was affable, loving and surprisingly calm. He really had to have been 'on something' the last time I saw him, I concluded.

I gradually grew more confident that he would not run away from me this time and asked him whether he fancied a cup of coffee. He nodded but added that he was absolutely starving and his feet were killing him with all the walking he had done over the last couple of days. He said he hadn't eaten a thing for the best part of a day and, judging from his general appearance, I could well believe him. I made him a few slices of cheese on toast to go with his coffee. I then asked him calmly why he hadn't rung to reassure me as I had only wanted to know that he was safe. His reply indicated to me that he had been in a paranoid state. He was convinced that the police were constantly tracking his whereabouts through his mobile phone signal and his fears grew so strong that he decided to bury his device in someone's front garden in Lytham. He could no longer remember the house number or even the name of the street where he had deposited it. The mobile was never recovered.

It was now 6am and I was faced with a big decision to make. I knew if I attempted to contact the police with Chris in such close proximity to me it would unnerve him and he would run a mile. So I attempted to strike up a deal with him. I said that if I was to treat him to a trip to McDonald's for a 'big breakfast' would he allow me to drive him back to the hospital immediately afterwards? He bought my 'meal deal' offer without a second thought and I reckoned that this was for two reasons. He was still feeling ravenous for a start because my two slices of cheesy toast at about 3am had not really hit the mark. And secondly, I formed the distinct impression that he was sick and tired of being a fugitive on the run. I was sure that he was more than ready to return to a lovely warm room on his ward and have a good, long rest.

I did feel that I was betraying the police in some way by doing things my way and for not keeping them 'in the loop'. But I knew Chris as well as anyone and I was certain that my cunning plan would do the trick. And it worked an absolute treat. I had him duly returned to the ward by 8am, complete with a full stomach, almost three full days after he had first absconded. The hospital staff were delighted with his return and congratulated me for doing a sterling job. The police were also naturally well pleased with the outcome. And there were no questions asked about how I had managed to bring the matter to a satisfactory conclusion.

As expected, I never managed to recover my gleaming bike. Chris said he had no idea where he had left it, or dumped it, and

I was inclined to believe him, given his highly suspect mental state at the time. Nevertheless, I felt that it was a small price to pay now that he was back in safe hands once again

There is a footnote to this long, drawn-out drama. I had evidently been somewhat premature with my confident early morning assertion that Chris was 'ready for a return to hospital for a long rest'. On that very same day, 25 March, I was informed that he had attempted to escape yet again and managed to wreak more havoc, having smashed a door on the ward and needing to be forcibly restrained. I'm sure the ward staff realised then, if not before, that they had a real handful on their hands.

Thank Goodness I didn't know at the time that during the course of the next ten years, a further thirty 'escape dramas' would be chalked up against Chris's name. And we would somehow have to deal with them all in the best way we possibly could.

CHAPTER 5
Those Turbulent Twenties
2008 – 2015

A large majority of mental health disorders emerge during adolescence or when people reach their early twenties. With anxiety disorders there's about a 90% chance that this will start to show itself as an adolescent. Recent research suggests that adolescence is a time when the brain is changing to a great degree. Apparently, it was once thought that the brain didn't change that much after earlier childhood, but it now seems that the brain continues to undergo really some really big changes up until one is in his early twenties. This is not set in stone by any means because different influences in a social environment can really have a profound impact, either positively or negatively, on the way we eventually turn out.

It also seems that the mental health disorders that people suffer in their twenties do gradually dissipate. Sadly, this has not been the case with Chris; his continuing poor mental health may have been attributable to questionable social habits during the period referred to above. That is, during the times he was free, and in the community, which sadly was not too often.

As we have already noted in the previous chapter, Chris's early twenties got off to a dreadful start and we pick up the story now on 9 April 2009 when he was formally detained under Section 3 of the Mental Health Act 1983. There was no disputing the decision especially in the wake of the chaos he had caused during the mammoth escape debacle a few weeks earlier.

As if his novel notoriety wasn't enough already, on 15 April he managed to abscond once again from the ward's secure garden and vanish into thin air before the staff had an opportunity to nab him. But unlike on his previous occasion, this time was notable only for its brevity. He was spotted by police a couple of hours later on Church Street as headed in the direction of Blackpool's town centre, and was swiftly returned to base with a minimum amount of fuss. But he had well and truly set out his stall as a serial escape artist in the making. And in the years that followed this certainly proved to be the case.

After this latest brief episode, he was watched like a hawk and given no further opportunities to do a runner. His behaviour actually settled down nicely after all his early shenanigans. He was accepted by the Lancashire Early Intervention Service in late April, and discharged from his section. He came back home to us in Lytham on 1 June.

The Early Intervention Service is a multidisciplinary team which supports young people who are experiencing a first episode of psychosis. The team comprises staff from a variety of disciplines including nursing, social work, occupational therapy and psychology. Their aims are to help people who have experiences that are distressing and hard to make any real sense of, which can sometimes lead to psychosis. And to give them the right help and support early on so that they can carry on with their lives as normally as possible.

It could have gone better for Chris if he had been able to latch onto the EIS before he was hospitalised but we thought it was better late than never. And I have to say that their team was fantastic in helping Chris through those early difficult and unpleasant times. They were regular visitors to our home and gave Chris endless support, guidance and advice. But once he had suffered a relapse and was returned to hospital, their involvement in his care unfortunately had to end.

Having read this far, you may be wondering exactly which medical conditions that my son actually suffers from. I have deliberately not mentioned this until now because we have received so many likely diagnoses over the years from health professionals that we have had some difficulty keeping up with them all. We were advised initially that he suffered from a condition known as bipolar disorder, and this diagnosis has been considered accurate by everyone right through to the present day. The condition was formerly known as manic depressive which is characterised by extreme mood changes that can swing from extremely high to extremely low. And in Chris's case these mood variations can occur very rapidly indeed. He has said to me so many times that he craves his 'high' moods because it makes him feel almost invincible. He was soon prescribed a suitable mood stabilising medication and, had he continued to take this religiously each day, this problem may have been kept largely at bay. But alas, Chris has never been fully compliant over the years with his prescribed medications and inevitable setbacks have occurred.

Over the years we have also received a number of diagnoses which range from hebephrenic schizophrenia, paranoid schizophrenia, borderline personality disorder (or BPD) and there has even been a suggestion that he may be placed somewhere on the autism spectrum. Hebephrenic schizophrenia has become the longest prevailing diagnosis and the following description of the condition does seem to, more or less, fit Chris.

Another term for the above condition is disorganised schizophrenia and is typified by shallow and inappropriate emotional responses, foolish or sometimes bizarre behaviour.

Also evident can be false beliefs (or delusions) and false perceptions (or hallucinations). A person with this condition is likely to have difficulty beginning a specific task such as starting to cook and prepare a meal and may also have difficulties in finishing a task. It is associated with early onset, usually between the ages of eighteen to twenty-five. Not all of the above symptoms can be attributed to Chris but some of the other elements most certainly can.

About three weeks after he had returned home it became clear that Chris was failing to be compliant with his medication and he started to drink more than the odd drop of alcohol, which he was cautioned against on leaving hospital. Alcohol can have serious detrimental effects for those who are prescribed a complex concoction of medications, such as those that Chris takes.

It was only a matter of one more week, on 26 June, that he was back in the Parkwood unit at Blackpool Victoria hospital and was once again detained under a Section 3.

News then emerged, a week later, that prior to his latest re-admission he was arrested for driving a car without a licence and insurance. There was no suggestion that he had taken the car without permission but the offences were bad enough as they were.

Chris had taken several driving tests in the past but had failed them all. He was, however, quite proficient at driving tractors as he had worked on his granddad's farm for long periods during his school holidays. It was decided, some months later, that no further action was to be taken regarding the driving offences because he was considered to be mentally ill at the time.

Just two months later, on 14 September, he was released from hospital again. A Community Treatment Order was considered, which would mean that he would be required to comply with certain conditions or run the risk of being returned to hospital. But although the option was given every consideration, no application was eventually made.

All this zigzagging in and out of hospital every few months was not doing anyone any favours and we decided to made enquiries as to whether he might be able to take a course of some sort which would reduce the likelihood of him being readmitted. As a result of our persistence, a course of Cognitive Behavioural Therapy (or CBT for short) began on 13 November and we kept our fingers crossed that this might help to put him back on the right track. This proved to be successful but only to a limited extent due to Chris's indifferent level of engagement whilst on the course.

During his last short period in hospital, it was reported to me by ward staff that he had occasionally self-harmed. This was already clear to me anyway, because whenever I visited,+ he was more than happy to show me his forearms which often showed nasty criss-crossed messes of cuts. Several of these cuts could probably be best described as little more than scratches but, nevertheless, it was an ominous and disturbing new development.

Life returned to some sort of normality following his latest discharge and I was tempted to think that Christmas 2009 might be a happy and relaxing festive period for our family. He was experiencing a few residual symptoms of psychosis but we understood that these would gradually fade away once he began to engage in leisure and other activities and could focus his mind on the wider world that had newly opened up to him.

This theory turned out to be accurate as he was to enjoy more than eighteen months of hospital-free existence. It was probably the best and most satisfying period of time he was destined to have in the whole of his twenties. One example of this occurred in May 2010 when Chris, Hannah and myself had the amazing experience of seeing our local football team win promotion to the Premier League. We defeated Cardiff City by three goals to two at Wembley Stadium in front of a full capacity attendance on a wonderfully warm day. We spent the whole weekend together in London and had a simply unforgettable time. The memories of that weekend will remain with us forever, not least because it remains the very last time that the three of us have spent an extended period of time together. We now had a season of Premiership football to look forward to and this would definitely give Chris, and indeed us all, plenty to focus our minds on.

During the following week as Blackpool FC's homecoming party took place on the town's Promenade, Chris applied to take part in a Princes Trust course which would run for several weeks, if he was successful. This is a youth charity that helps young people who are aged between 11 and 30 to get into employment. I saw this was a superb opportunity for Chris to show what he was made of and he might even land himself a good job at the end of the course, we hoped. I attended the interview for his enrolment onto the course with Chris to offer a little moral support and a few tips for when it was his turn to be interviewed. I coached him a little beforehand and advised him of a few positive points to bring up if he was able to. I also mentioned a few things that he should try to avoid saying.

The interview got underway and I sat quietly and unobtrusively at the back of the room. The man in charge began by giving Chris a short resume of himself and his career to date. He told Chris that he had recently been seconded to this Princes Trust role from his regular occupation in the police force. At this exact point Chris butted in and wagged a friendly finger at the interviewer. He then said to him with a giggle and a wry smile, 'I knew it. I just knew you were a bloody cop. I can smell one a mile away!'

Oh dear! I positively cringed and prayed that the floor would suddenly open up and devour me. A deathly hush pervaded throughout the room lasting for several seconds but seemed far longer.

'I think it would be best, Chris, if you were to go home and have a good think about whether you really want to be on this course,' he eventually replied.

And that was basically it. The interview was over. It was undoubtedly the shortest interview he had ever been involved in by a country mile — and was ever likely to be for that matter.

We drove home to Lytham in stunned silence. I knew that, in his own way, he had only tried to make light conversation with the pleasant interviewer chap but Chris's unique form of syntax was in overdrive and he could scarcely have made a bigger blunder if he had tried. And all that was with his very first sentence of the interview!

A day later, we received a telephone call from a Princes Trust official and were amazed to learn that Chris had been accepted for inclusion on the course. I was thrilled but extremely surprised while Chris seemed to be more relieved than anything else.

This signalled the start of a fantastic three months of activities and training for Chris with the Princes Trust. He especially enjoyed an outward-bound experience when he was sent on a residential week in the Lake district. He also formed some good friendships with other people on the course.

He was also given the chance to do two weeks' work experience in a local supermarket and he thoroughly enjoyed his time there, receiving good feedback from their management. It was fairly menial work, by all accounts, but he undertook all that was asked of him with gusto and plenty of uncharacteristic enthusiasm. I thought to myself, maybe supermarket work is something that Chris could have a good look at again at some stage in the future.

He completed his Princes Trust experience in late August and, at a presentation ceremony, he was proud to receive his Certificate, having successfully completed the course. But arguably more important than that, the whole adventure worked wonders for his self-confidence and his mental health too because he was given little spare time and so much to fully focus his mind on.

The two of us went to Majorca for a week in the sun the following month. It was as much a reward for Chris's sterling endeavours throughout the summer as it was for anything else. But it was so good for the two of us just to get away and relax — far away from the pressures of mental health and hospital care staff, excellent though a large majority of them undoubtedly are. I still had to ensure that he took his array of medications every day without fail. I also recognised the fact that he would probably be enjoying an occasional pint of beer and the very last thing I needed was for his health to take a nasty dip whilst we were out of the country.

It was early evening in sunny Majorca and we had scarcely unpacked our cases when Chris announced that he was going for a wander on the sea front, ostensibly to 'find his bearings'. He certainly found something whilst he wandered on his travels but it wasn't only his bearings. He told me he came across a guy who was selling 'weed' and the temptation proved too great and he couldn't pass on the opportunity. He arrived back in our hotel room with a vacant smile on his face and reeking of a horrible, musky odour. I decided that any more strolls along the sea front would be spent exclusively with me for the remainder of the week. But this minor episode aside, we had a brilliant time and it was a rare treat to see him laughing and joking so often. It also proved to be a treat for me as he took all his medication with a bare minimum of fuss which made my life so much easier.

Hannah had by now left the family nest and, at twenty-four years of age, she spent that summer working and living at Disneyland in Florida. Meanwhile, Chris and I spent plenty of quality time together which included several trips around the country following our football team to watch them play in some superb Premiership stadia for the very first time. In mid-November we stayed over in London after watching our team play out a goalless draw with West Ham United. It was a cold day and the match was not especially memorable but our weekend away definitely was, and again, his behaviour was impeccable. I had almost forgotten about those dark days of the past and felt I had justifiable cause to look toward to a happy future for both of us.

It was on one of the days between Christmas 2010 and the New Year that I met Sue who was to become my second wife a little less than a year later. We had known each other fairly well from our school days and we actually worked together several years later for a while in the civil service. Maybe this was always meant to be. I resolved to make the following year an excellent one for all of us and was sure that this would be the case.

I was wrong. The following year proved to be a bitter sweet one for me. Sue and I were happily married in the November but Chris's life went completely off the rails yet again and his life was back in unbridled chaos.

The new year had begun quietly enough and any thoughts of

another Chris relapse could not have been further from my mind. But by early May the Home Treatment team had begun to visit us after concerns about Chris's mental health had emerged. They did a valiant job trying to stem the seemingly inevitable tide of a return to psychosis but their fire-fighting was only to delay the inevitable. A week later, the countdown began for Chris and a re-admittance to hospital seemed just around the corner. He had completely trashed his bedroom in our house and then drove around Lytham on his motorbike whilst considerably intoxicated. And so, on the first day of June, he found himself back at Parkwood hospital.

He was admitted to the acute level ward and his Section 2 was duly upgraded to a Section 3 by the end of the month. His conduct soon proved to be so disruptive on the ward that he had to be transferred to the hospital's intensive care (PICU) ward.

In the next few months, we saw a veritable see-saw of transfers to and from various hospital wards; he even managed to squeeze in few more successful abscondings. I brought him back to the ward on each of his successful escapes with the help of a smattering of gentle coaxing, which I had become reasonably skilled at by then through these experiences. On one of these occasions, I found him lounging on open display in a local pub boozing merrily away. He promised he would return to the ward with me but only after I had enjoyed a few pints of beer with him!

There were punch ups on the wards too and Chris was always there or thereabouts in the mix of things. I continued to visit him every day throughout this awful spell of behaviour while, at the same time, doing my best to make final arrangements for our wedding which was fast approaching.

Chris was granted a full day's unescorted leave for our wedding. The venue for the ceremony and reception was a hotel

(De Vere) in east Blackpool which just happened to be no more than a few hundred metres away from Parkwood hospital where Chris was based at the time. He rose to the occasion magnificently and his short speech from the top table in front of so many people made me so proud as I'm sure it must have been difficult for him. A taxi arrived in the evening to take him back to his ward. By this time, he was a little worse for wear, alcohol-wise, but on this occasion, I suppose he had fully deserved it.

We were faced with an 'informal patient' situation a month later, a few days after Christmas. Chris had recognised the fact that the six-month term of Section 3 status had recently lapsed and decided to capitalise on this to the fullest degree. He confidently asked his nurse, in view of this, if he could now discharge himself and return home. A short-term compromise was reached and he was granted extended periods of leave which, ostensibly, would be to carefully monitor how he handled it all before judging his suitability for discharge. It was definitely an accident just waiting to happen, I thought to myself, especially with New Year's Eve just around the corner.

He did get up to a little mischief on the final day of 2011 but, all things considered, it could have been a good deal worse. He had decided to stay out for the entire day and evening in Lytham and it came as no surprise that he ended up quite drunk. He evidently didn't fancy a long trip back to his ward in Blackpool so he opted instead to come home to sleep at our house. I was already well in the land of nod when I was awakened by a loud shattering noise which sounded like breaking glass. I ran downstairs to find Chris in the kitchen ferreting around in the fridge for something to eat. I noticed that the floor tiles were heavily coated with a dusting of glass shards from the main window which he had broken to gain entry. A friend had been with him but wisely he disappeared into thin air once he realised that there had been some damage. Chris offered to pay me for a replacement window and this time I decided to take him up on the offer. I allowed him to sleep in his own bed for the remainder of the night before I drove him back to the ward the following morning. A brilliant opening to the New Year, I reflected wistfully.

Despite his horseplay on New Year's Eve, we were amazed, but very pleased, that only three weeks later he was discharged from his section and left hospital. As a temporary arrangement, he was found a bed in a St. Annes nursing home until one became available for him at the Richmond Fellowship facility, which was close by. He remained at the nursing home for five months, which was far longer than we had expected, and, unsurprisingly, he was the youngest resident in there by a country mile!

He was now based little more than a hundred metres from the beach and the Irish Sea. Little did he know then that he would spend a period of more than a year out of hospital, which was about as good as it was ever likely to get. We enjoyed many football 'kick abouts' on the beach, pub meals and several trips out. It was all smiles for quite a while as his mental health remained on an even keel.

He moved into the Richmond Fellowship in June but, before long, reports came to light that he might be using drugs again and he was watched closely from then onwards. He had so much freedom to come and go almost as he pleased but that seemed to be never quite enough for him and he soon resented the minor limitations that their policies imposed on him. There was no pleasing him apparently and he gradually became disillusioned with the place.

He informed his care team and care coordinator of his

intention to stop taking medication because he felt they were making him feel sluggish. He declined reviews with his consultant but later relented on this point and began to take his medication again. He said to me a number of times that cocaine made him feel 'healthy and alert' and because of this he considered that his other medications were no longer necessary. As the months drifted by, his thoughts constantly ebbed and flowed as to whether he might take his medications or not; sometimes he was inclined to take them and at other times he vehemently avoided them.

Mental health-wise, he was somehow managing to keep his head just above the water line and early in the new year he was offered the chance of some regular voluntary work at a charity shop situated around the corner from where he was based. He found the experience enjoyable and rewarding for a short while but he complained that he was being used only behind the scenes with menial duties and not given the chance to work on the actual shop floor. So another opportunity for him to do something worthwhile with his life had gone to the wall and he decided never to return.

By mid-summer his relationship with Richmond Fellowship was rapidly crumbling. He was having issues with another resident and he told his care coordinator and myself that he must be found new accommodation as a matter of some urgency. He added that he did not want a similar place to the Richmond Fellowship next time around. In other words, he felt he was more than capable of living independently. A number of options were examined over the course of the following month and we discussed them all at some length. I personally felt that a move to independent living would be a disastrous move for him. He would have little daily help and support, other than from myself, if he managed to get his way. And, as usual he did finally get his own way.

His new home was a top floor flat situated only half a mile from the Richmond Fellowship home he had just left. It was a fairly dismal looking flat, somewhat gloomy and rather old fashioned. If I was to crane my neck upwards from the front window, I had a partial view of the Irish Sea in the distance. I suppose that represented something of a minor saving grace. It wasn't long before his moods were as gloomy as the flat, he had just taken over. I visited him each day to keep a firm eye on things and to keep on top of his daily needs. It was not a happy time for any of us, but especially so for Chris. On a wing and a prayer, he somehow managed to remain in his flat for another six months.

It wasn't long afterwards that he began to be plagued by thoughts of suicide. He had brought up the subject with me a couple of times in the past, but only in the vaguest of terms, so it did not give me too much cause for concern then. But his rhetoric had changed for the worse, and he spoke of 'worthlessness' and 'not really wanting to be here any more'. He had self-harmed a little in the past, as we have already noted, but this was a completely different ball game.

Some years ago, I successfully completed an 'ASIST' course of training to learn more about this very difficult subject. Applied Suicide Intervention Skills Training is an interactive workshop course and it teaches participants to recognise when someone may have thoughts of suicide. The ASIST method helps reduce suicidal feelings in those at risk and is a cost-effective way to help address the problem of suicide. Once trained, it enables people to understand the reasons behind thoughts of suicide and also reasons for living. It also helps to helps to develop plans to increase levels of safety of people who find themselves at a risk of suicide.

I found the course absorbing and highly informative but often quite harrowing as well. I feel reasonably competent enough now to deal with a situation of this nature, if one unfortunately was to ever arise. But when one's own son is the subject of the problem most of the text book information flies straight out of the window. Once a close family member has become the subject, the huge emotional attachment largely overrides the majority of the training taught in the classroom.

I have spent many hours over the last several years comforting and coaxing Chris, attempting to ease him away from having these terrible feelings and guiding him into safer areas. Despite the many occasions he has spoken about suicide he has never actually attempted to follow through with it. As a family, we feel that he almost always raises the subject of suicide to maintain our attention and as a means of establishing some control over us. We invariably offer constant emotional support and guidance and even though we are 99% confident that he would never carry out his threat one ignores this entirely at one's peril. It could be that the one in a hundred chance is the one that he intends to execute the awful plan. And it matters not one jot whether he ever spoke of suicide to me in a flippant and matter of fact way, which was fairly often. I invariably treated every single one of his threats very seriously indeed because, had I simply brushed it off and made light of it to him, it could have given him the final kick and urge to go on and actually carry out the act.

We successfully weathered the immediate storm and he gradually spoke less and less about suicide and the associated subject of self-harm. But our vigilance levels remained on red alert at all times and we stayed 'on guard' right through to the present day.

In fact, he gave us little further cause for worry for the rest of the year and we were relieved that there was no need to press the panic button. Only one black cloud was starting to appear on the horizon and that was Chris's determination to move north to live in Scotland all alone 'in about six months' time'. He started to mention his idea first of all in September 2013 and so, by the early part of the following year, we held our breaths and prayed that he had either forgotten all about it or had thought better of the whole idea in the meantime. Unfortunately, we learned that it was still very much on his mind and he was keen to go ahead with it.

When March arrived Chris made it crystal clear to me that he would be off to Scotland soon — to live in the western island of Stornoway to be precise. I was naturally dead set against it and I thought it was an extremely silly idea for so many reasons and I repeatedly told him so.

'Please, Chris, give me just one good reason why you would possibly want to live up there? It's very cold for one thing and you'd be so far away from all your family,' I pleaded.

'I've been looking at lots of books, Dad, and it sounds great to me,' he replied.

'I think you'd find the reality of it would be completely different to simply looking at some nice photos in books. Don't you agree, Chris?'

'I'm thinking of buying my own lake up there and filling it up with salmon so I can just pull them out and cook them when I'm hungry. I might also get some sharks and put them in there as well.' I had always known that he loved eating all sorts of fish but this was pie in the sky nonsense and he was clearly in a delusional state.

'I'll tell you what, Chris. How about if I go with you by train up north as far as Inverness? We could spend a few days there together and you'd then be able to get a feel for the area. And then, if you don't like it you can come home with me.

'Yeah, okay. I can go with that deal, Dad,' was his surprisingly pleasing reply.

The subject of his move up north never raised its head again which I thought was somehow ominous. Did he have another trick up his sleeve, I wondered? Fittingly, it was on April Fool's Day that I found out the answer. I received a phone call from Chris informing me that he was on a fast train, having just left Carlisle station and that he would ring me again when he had reached Inverness! He also threw in, for good measure, that he was already on his second malt whiskey. I was completely speechless. What on earth had happened to the deal we had struck so recently? I was beyond angry but tried hard not to show it because I knew that if I had ranted at him, his mood would very likely have changed quite dramatically and most probably for the worse. So I chose to say very little.

He rang me again as his train arrived in Inverness. He told me that it was freezing cold there and that he had not taken a coat with him. His speech appeared a little slurred too and I guessed that he hadn't stopped at just the two malts. I thanked him for letting me know he had arrived in one piece and pleaded with him to be so careful and to keep in touch regularly. It was a very worrying time for many reasons, not least because he had taken along with him only a limited amount of medication. This was worse than his major absconding incidents because he was now in a completely unfamiliar place, his mental health was clearly unstable and, to cap it all, he was three sheets to the wind. That wasn't a wonderful combination by any stretch of the imagination.

I have to say that the Inverness news blackout that followed ranked with some of my most difficult hours in living memory. It was all well and good being an escapee from local hospital and popping into a pub or two but he was now actually in a different country!

I didn't have much longer to wait until he unveiled his next instalment. He rang again but sounded in one heck of a state. He was crying incessantly and, in between tears, all he could manage to say was it had all been such a horrible mistake and that he would be on the next train back to Lancashire in the morning. He promised me he would check into a local hotel to thaw out and try to 'sleep everything off until the morning'. I said I would keep ringing him from 6am to make sure he wouldn't miss his train. I felt like having a few whiskies myself but, this time, in celebration as he would soon be homeward bound.

He did not raid the malt whiskey bottle on his return journey; strong coffees were very much the order of the day. He was fairly quiet and a little maudlin during our frequent chats as he headed south fast. His mobile ran out of juice just as his train ripped through Cumbria — and unfortunately, he hadn't remembered to take a charger with him!

I did have a rough idea about when his train would be due back in town and I also had one or two thoughts about where he might head once he was back in town. It was all pure guesswork because we had lost our only line of communication. But sure enough, I found him where I imagined he would be — slumped on a bench in his local shopping area and half asleep. He was so relieved to be back home and promised me faithfully, there and then, that he would never, ever do this again. This was one extremely tough lesson learned, I thought to myself, but there was no serious harm done — other than to my blood pressure.

The months of April and May 2014 were tumultuous times for Chris as he edged ever closer to a relapse and a further spell of hospitalisation.

As Chris's nearest relative, I stayed in close contact with his care coordinator throughout the next crucial period as fresh developments were occurring very often. His aborted trip to Scotland had given him a firm reality check; he now recognised his own considerable limitations when he was on his own and it shocked and upset him. This seemed to be the catalyst for a series of rash and ill-judged decisions.

He bought a car from some place in Blackpool and, notwithstanding the fact that he hadn't passed his test and was uninsured, he drove it back and parked it outside his flat. It has often puzzled me as to why garage owners do not ask potential buyers for evidence of valid driver's licences before they proceed to sell on a car. He did promise me, however, that he would not drive it again and assured me that it was parked outside, purely 'for show' and for 'something to tinker about with and clean every week'. I discovered that the car tax was still valid so that was a minor saving grace.

It was reported by his care coordinator in the middle of April that Chris had started to close himself off from almost everyone. He continued to see me but began to regard all care workers with a good deal of suspicion. He could probably sense that the net was beginning to close in on him and he knew only too well where he would then be heading. He declined all attempts to have a Mental Health Assessment (until much later) and, although he agreed to a referral from the Home Treatment Team, he steadfastly resisted all efforts after that to allow anyone near his flat.

On a rare day of his lucidity, he agreed to visit his consultant and was swiftly driven there by his care coordinator before Chris had the time to suggest that they could use his own car. He was clearly presenting with symptoms indicating relapse and two new medications were prescribed in a last-ditch attempt to head off the risk of even further deterioration. He was given Zopiclone as a sleeping aid as he was wide awake for long periods. He was also given Aripiprazole, or Abilify, an antipsychotic drug which is used primarily in the treatment of schizophrenia and bipolar disorder. On the first day that he took his new medication he took two Zopiclone tablets instead of one and it was uncertain as to whether this was a genuine mistake or deliberate. He was then under very close observation. That is, on the isolated occasions that he allowed the Home Treatment Team or anyone else to enter the flat. The Home Treatment Team's involvement was seen as a less restrictive option to hospital admission and it really was the last throw of the dice for him. If this did not reap dividends then there would be no alternative other than for him to be hospitalised.

On 14 May, a Mental Health Act Assessment was completed and Chris was admitted to Parkwood hospital and put into their acute ward again. And a week later he had his first taste on a PICU ward when he was moved there following a spell of unruly behaviour.

It was while Chris was on the PICU ward that I took part in my own unique version of a visit-athon! During the autumn and early winter, of 2014, I visited Chris every day for a period of almost four months. It wasn't a conscious thing but the longer my unbroken run continued the more it became almost a way of life and Chris expected it of me. There were other reasons for this extended run of visits. He was on a ward where he had precious few opportunities to have any periods of leave and was, therefore, fed up for much of the time. My visits often had the effect of 'breaking the day up' and cheering him up. Additionally, I cycled to Parkwood every day and this gradually morphed into a determined attempt to improve my fitness levels to some degree before my run was over.

It did come to an abrupt close one day in early December after I came a real cropper by hitting a patch of black ice. I was on my way to see him when I fell awkwardly and hurt my right hip and leg quite badly. The front wheel of my bike was pretty mangled in the mishap and it was rendered out of action. I struggled to my feet and managed to limp as far as a nearby park bench where I decided to ring Chris and tell him my bad news.

'Hi, Chris, it's me. I've had a bit of an accident on my bike on my way to see you. I've really hurt my leg and hip and they're absolutely wrecking me. My bike's in a right old mess as well and I can't ride it.'

'Oh, that's sad, Dad. But what time will you be coming then?'

'I'm going to have to give it a miss today because I can hardly walk,' I replied, my voice breaking up with pain as I spoke.

'What? But you always visit, Dad. Please, come on — you've just gotta come!'

My visiting run was at a close at long last but I still manage a smile now when I recall Chris's plaintive plea for me to put in an appearance despite my accident and injuries!

He remained on the PICU ward, for more than eight months in total, over Christmas and into the early part of 2015. He was deemed to be well enough by 17 February to be transferred to a rehabilitation unit named Newton House which is no more than a stone's throw away from Blackpool's Victoria hospital. This was his first attempt at rehabilitation but it most certainly would not be his last.

The full name of Chris's new temporary home is Newton House Recovery and Treatment Centre. It provides locked rehabilitation and treatment to individuals living with complex and enduring mental health conditions. He was so glad to be away from Parkwood after such a painfully long stint and he saw this as an ideal opportunity to be freed from the limitations imposed by Section 3 wards. He failed to realise that it was a locked rehabilitation unit and when he learned about it he was greatly annoyed until a modicum of acceptance kicked in much later. He felt he was back at square one despite my encouraging words that he was only one step away from complete freedom if he came through this test successfully. He remained unconvinced. It wasn't destined then to be the brightest of starts to his rehabilitation career.

There were many trials and tribulations during the five months he spent at Newton House. The psychologist had difficulty getting him to fully engage in any of his sessions after a reasonably encouraging start. Chris still held the belief that he was being held there under protest and as some kind of imposed penalty. The long and short of it was that he would remain 'locked in' and this continued to rankle with him.

There were some compensations for him at Newton House that made life more bearable. They organised five-a-side football sessions at a nearby Sports Centre which he relished; he had the chance to rekindle some of the special skills he'd learned whilst at school. There were also day trips to various countryside locations which Chris usually took full advantage of. That is, if he was able to get himself out of bed before the minibus left. He was now sleeping for England which was a far cry from the bad old days of a year ago when he had difficulty getting much sleep at all in the flat. The staff were excellent throughout his stay at Newton House and did their utmost to keep all the patients happy and reasonably content with their lives.

No story would ever be complete without the subject of Chris's ubiquitous escape antics raising its head. And his new hospital proved to be no exception to the rule. He managed to elude members of staff three times and vanish each time from sight and gain some temporary freedom. The first two instances were straightforward examples of running away, heading for the nearest pub, getting half plastered and returning to base under his own steam. And he then had to face the music which usually resulted in his leave privilege being suspended for a while. We will learn about his third and final incident, which was a far less savoury episode, a little later on.

Sandwiched in between, he was granted generous amounts of escorted leave with a member of staff. I often went along with the two of them and so there was a party of three of us who often used to wander along the Blackpool seafront and take advantage of the bracing seaside air. He used these periods of leave sensibly and caused us no real problems. Well, that is other than one new emerging problem. One day he asked his escort if he could have a quick look in a local betting office we had just spotted because these places had always fascinated him. He had had little involvement with 'bookies' and gambling in the past so we thought it wouldn't do too much harm if he had a quick peep in.

I have not referred to the following issue until now but the aforementioned scenario allows me with the perfect opportunity to raise it. Chris undoubtedly has an addictive personality, which means he has personality traits that make him more prone to developing addictions. This has caused us varying degrees of grief in the past dependent upon how serious the specific addiction is. Someone who has an addictive personality tends to spend excessive amounts of time on certain behaviours. Chris can latch on to something new and novel very quickly indeed, if he is sufficiently attracted to it, and can easily become fixated. The subject of gambling had raised its head and it became the most recent object of his addiction — and affection.

Once we had entered the betting office Chris was instantly drawn to the roulette machine and made a direct beeline to it. He began to feed five-pound notes into the machine and off he went. His new 'career' had begun.

The worst thing that could have possibly happened that day did actually happen — he proceeded to win a whole packet of money. He left the place half an hour later with a huge grin on his face and equally huge bulging pockets. Once he was back at Newton House, he couldn't help but tell everyone how incredibly easy it was to make quick easy cash and how he couldn't wait to get back there to get back on the winning trail again.

Well, I'm sure you can imagine how everything panned out over the course of the days and weeks that followed. His early stash of profit was soon swallowed up by the machine together with a good deal more besides. But his obsession with this kind of machine was set to rumble on and on for years to come. That is, when he was out of hospital.

His time at Newton House ended ignominiously and swiftly at the tail end of July. It came about as a direct result of his third attempt to escape. He had made a sudden dart into the garden area, and whilst attempting to scale a fence which separated him from the outside world and freedom, he was grabbed by two members of staff. A scuffle ensued but he was still able to scramble over the fence and to vanish. Unfortunately, the two members of staff who attempted to apprehend him were injured in the fracas. Chris returned to the unit not long afterwards having probably realised the gravity of his situation and exactly what had happened to the staff members.

The following morning my son was transferred to the Harbour Hospital which is situated on the outskirts of Blackpool. There was to be no fanfare or fond farewells — he just slipped quietly away. It would be Chris's first visit at the newly-opened facility, where he would remain until 5 November. It would not, however, be his last time at the Harbour on his journey by any means.

CHAPTER 6
Dad's Role and his Life in the Caring Community

It was a hot and sunny day in mid-August 2015 that it first dawned on me that I could actually be termed a carer. At the time, my son was twelve months into his third hospital stint in five years, each time detained under Section 3 of the Mental Health Act. He was an inpatient on an acute level ward at the Harbour Hospital in Blackpool this time. The hospital has a favourable location just a little more than a mile and a half from where I live. This close proximity allowed me the opportunity to visit him very frequently. In fact, more often than not, I called in to visit Chris five or six times a week. The ward staff often wagged me about my regular visiting attendance and many times suggested that it might be a good idea if I was to bring my own bed along!

On this particular morning I had arrived at the ward armed, as usual, with my trusty notebook and other bits and bobs of relevant information. This would hopefully enable me to speak and act, as always, in Chris's best interests at a CPA meeting. To give this commonly used abbreviation its Sunday name, it is a 'Care Programme Approach'. The CPA is a framework which is used to assess the patient's needs and, under this type of meeting, his or her care coordinator should be present to monitor care and support.

I was keyed up as usual and ready for the fray. I often felt that these occasions were almost tantamount to 'us' and 'them' affairs. I had always harboured (no pun intended) more than a modicum of anxiety at these meetings because, as a lay person as opposed to a professional, I often felt I played the role of an extra. I seldom felt listened to when I raised relevant points and sometimes my comments were completely glossed over. It seemed that suggestions and ideas that I threw into the melting pot for discussion were summarily overlooked. This point has been endorsed by many carers that I've come to know over the years on the occasions we have shared our respective caring experiences. I'm sure that many of you reading this will agree, that in many ways, parents, nearest relatives, close friends and other family members can often have vital snippets of highly relevant information about their loved ones that they would be more than delighted to share if it would help in any way.

With this background established, the aforementioned meeting duly went ahead. I learned that Chris's regular care coordinator had tendered his apologies earlier as he was unavailable on the day. A deputy 'AMHP', whom I had not previously met, acted as his stand in. By way of explanation, AMHP is an abbreviation which stands for Approved Mental Health Professional. These people hold one of the most important and senior professional roles in the whole of the mental health services. They operate across a number of services, over twenty-four hours a day, and work alongside many other professionals in similar fields. The role is challenging and legally accountable and I have found in my own experiences all the above points to be true. Most of the AMHPs that I have come across and had dealings with over the years have done first class jobs.

Forty-five minutes later, the meeting drew to a close and I was conscious throughout that the deputising care co-ordinator had been observing me. I was proved correct because he took me aside, smiled warmly and said to me with sincerity, 'Rob, I've been watching you during the meeting and you looked a little stressed to me and I felt you might be under some pressure. I hope you don't mind me saying so but I you may benefit from a little help at the moment. What do you think? Do you agree?'

My initial reaction was one of mild indignation. I was a little rattled already by what I had heard during the meeting so I responded in a dismissive fashion but courteously, 'I'm sure I'm coping well enough at the moment, thanks. No problems to report but I appreciate your concern.'

The gentleman nodded back to me respectfully and decided not to pursue the conversation any longer at that stage.

I reckoned that as I had been looking after Chris well enough for most of his life up to that point, why on earth would I suddenly require the help, support and assistance of anyone else? I discovered in the fullness of time that my initial reaction was wrong and seriously misplaced. I also learned, as a direct result of my serendipitous meeting with this guy, that personal pressures, stress levels and anxiety often have a sneaky habit of creeping up quietly on oneself. And, as one can appreciate, this can cause alarm bells to ring and may turn out to be dangerous to one's health. I refused, or at least could not accept those beliefs, in the early days of my caring journey.

I was probably a typical example of what some might rightly term a 'man thing'. Some guys, including quite a few I know personally, never seem to allow their shields to slip and let their feelings rise naturally to the surface. In other words, some think that it's better to stand strong, maintain a 'stiff upper lip' and, as a consequence, tend to bottle things up. Some guys often won't admit to themselves, or completely disregard the fact, that they may have deep-seated underlying problems which can lurk around in one's deep background. I appreciate now that a least some of these emotions could quite easily have been attributed to me and I'd like to think that I address them now in a more positive way. This is largely courtesy of the help, support and guidance I've received during my long period as a carer.

The care coordinator clearly noted my slightly irksome response to his suggestion but, as we were leaving the room, he handed a card to me on which he had jotted a name and a phone number. He suggested that I might like to give these people a buzz one day as they could well be of some value to me. I took a cursory glance at the card and saw the name 'The Blackpool Carers Centre', an organisation that I had never come across before — or even heard of for that matter. I thanked him perfunctorily for the card and for his valuable input at the meeting and we went our separate ways. I have never met this man again after that day but I often recall my brief chat with some affection. I promptly tucked the small card away in my wallet, and I didn't really give it a further thought until a few weeks later.

When I did eventually decide to ring the number that was written on the card, I soon found myself enjoying a warm and friendly conversation with a member of staff at the Blackpool Carers Centre. The upshot of the call was that I was cordially invited to go along to one of the Centre's Peer Support Group meetings, without any obligation, and 'just see how it goes from there'.

Even after this pleasant telephone conversation I was still far from convinced that support groups, meetings and all that went along with them were the right move for me. I already attend enough meetings to sink a proverbial battleship, I reasoned. Nevertheless, despite my ambivalence, I decided to turn up to the carers' meeting as I promised I would.

I still had no idea at all what a 'Peer Support Group' was,

what they got up to or what I was likely to expect there. But I went along with a completely open mind and decided that, even in a worst-case scenario, it would amount only to a waste of a single morning of my time. As events transpired, it wasn't a waste of time or a flop at all as I was pleasantly surprised to discover that I was thoroughly absorbed in what I heard and thoroughly enjoyed the experience. I learned, to my surprise, that there were so many other local people who were in similar caring situations to my own. It didn't take long for the general buzz and chatter around a large oval shaped oak table to strike a rich chord with me.

And I somehow had always thought that I might be almost one of a kind in my particular situation!

Over the course of the next few months, I shared my own caring experiences with the group and it proved beneficial to me in a number of ways. I noticed that most of the carers at my first meeting were having a good old moan amongst themselves about their own particular woes, grievances and predicaments. And it became clear to me that, as a result of unloading many things from their chests, the burdens that they were carrying around were being eased, albeit temporarily. It was truly a new and cathartic experience for me. I listened intently to the lively chatter but on that first visit, as I was fairly shy at the time, I made no meaningful contribution to the conversation. I listened only but that was quite enough for me. A common thread amongst the banter centred around the others' perceived frailties of the mental health system and several of its employees. To be more specific, it was apparent that the whole system including doctors, consultants, social workers and a myriad of other care workers in the community were causing them plenty of angst and letting them down in various ways. There were obviously no immediate solutions to everyone's problems but the mere act of talking about their grievances was clearly having an uplifting impact on all and sundry. And as much as anything else that I saw and heard at that first meeting, it was so reassuring to learn that there was so much help out there in the community if it was ever needed.

I had now turned full circle from my original stance and in double fast time too. I left my original indifference well behind me and found myself almost counting down the days until I could attend the next meeting.

As the weeks and months drifted by, I gradually began to immerse myself in activities at the Carers Centre. And meanwhile, Chris was improving nicely in hospital but still not quite ready for discharge from his section. A few more weeks should be long enough do the trick, I thought, but one could never be absolutely certain as health professionals can often have a totally different take on things.

I soon started to feel a warm part of this new world that had suddenly opened up before me. And sandwiched in between all the activity was, of course, my regular visits to see Chris. It was a constant battle to keep his spirits up and, although I encouraged him, as much I was able to, it was never easy. It was only at around this time that I began to truly realise that I was actually a carer. And I have to say that I was surprisingly content with the tag. I had unknowingly been a carer all along, for a good, many years, without ever regarding myself as such.

I was fortunate enough to make a number of friends at the Carers Centre and began to feel more confident and composed within myself. I found that I was able to cope more easily with whatever life could throw at me. And there was plenty of it flying around — and still is! Life was never going to be easy but it was starting to be much less of a struggle and I looked forward to the challenges ahead with more strength.

I decided that it was high time I did something worthwhile to repay the Centre in some way. So I decided to undertake a charity venture on their behalf and challenged myself to take on a solo 'Coast to Coast' cycle trip across England. The promenade at Morecambe Bay on the Irish Sea coastline would be my designated start point and my trek would take me over the Pennine hills and through to Bridlington on the east coast of Yorkshire and the North Sea. I had already been a keen cyclist for a number of years and saw this as a perfect opportunity to push my own boundaries to a higher level. My main objective was, of course, to raise as much cash as I possibly could for the benefit of the Carers Centre, by whatever means that I could. I opened a *Just Giving* account online and hoped that donations would soon come rolling in.

So what exactly is the Carers Centre all about and what do they strive to achieve in the local Blackpool community? They are an independent charity and a network partner of the Carers Trust, a nationwide charity. Sadly, there are literally thousands of carers based in the Blackpool area. Their caring roles could be due to a whole array of factors which include age, physical or mental illness, substance misuse or disability.

The Blackpool Carers Centre provides a range of services which are designed to support and enhance the lives of unpaid carers of all ages throughout the town and the Fylde Coast. They host a range of support groups and organise many activities for all age groups including occasional mini trips away. In fact, my wife Sue and I enjoyed a pleasant three day 'respite' break to the Isle of Man in the Spring of 2017. This treat was offered to us free of all charge, courtesy of the Carers Centre.

We stayed in the small, quaint town of Ramsay along with

many other carers from all over the north west of England. The weather on the island was quite chilly as was still only early Spring time but we refused to let such a small matter affect our enjoyment one jot. There were lots more caring-related conversations over there on the island and everyone had their own unique and interesting experiences to relate. Several months down the line from my introduction to my new world in the caring fraternity, I was now able to make worthwhile contributions of my own during the lively discussions. I have to say that not everything that we chatted about were substandard reviews or horror stories about their treatment, the NHS service or their lives in general by any means. Maybe the pleasant and relaxed surroundings of our attractive hotel had the effect of mellowing our moods somewhat — or perhaps it was the alcohol!

So after a few months of arduous cycle training (I was a reasonably fit sixty-three years old at the time), the day of reckoning finally arrived. It was late April 2016 as I set off, all alone, on the long trek with my trusty racing bike over the steep Pennines and well beyond. Or at least it was my hope that my bike was going to prove 'trusty'. My wife drove me over to Morecambe (I was so pleased not to add an additional forty miles journey on my bike to reach the start point). I was itching to get started, my bike as well, which was stored away in the boot of our car. To cut a long and arduous story short, I did manage to make it successfully over to my destination on the opposite side of the country, and in one piece too. I completed the challenge in about twenty-four hours, with an excellent night's sleep in Ripon sandwiched in between. But more importantly, I managed to raise almost £1,000 for my chosen into the bargain. I must admit that the two of us (the bike and myself) took the far easier cross-country route home to Blackpool's North station courtesy of

British Rail!

Soon after the cycling episode had ended and I was fully recovered, I was asked whether I would like to take over the facilitation of our Carers' Peer Support group. It was the group that I had so tentatively dipped my toes into only twelve months previously. The support group is named 'HUGS', which is an acronym for Help, Understanding and Group Support. I jumped at the surprise opportunity and, over the course of the next few years, I think we all enjoyed some wonderful times together. We organised day trips now and again which continued to boost our spirits and energise us. It was pleasing that our group gradually grew in numbers to in excess of twenty regular attendees. We were never able to spirit away our difficulties into thin air but the act of talking, listening, sharing and laughing went a long, long way. 'A problem shared is a problem halved' really does ring absolutely true in the context of carers' lives in the community.

We were thrilled to learn that Chris had finally been discharged from his section in hospital and had moved temporarily into a Rest Home in Ansdell. His main move would be into a Richmond Fellowship facility in Ansdell, a small town just a few miles south of Blackpool, but he would have to wait a little longer until a vacancy became available there.

Richmond Fellowship is a National Mental Health Charity which strives to make full recovery from mental illness a reality. As an assisted accommodation facility, it enables people to actively take part in decisions about their support and to have as much control over this support as possible.

Now that Chris was out of hospital, I found myself juggling time between a settled home life, caring and attending to Chris's needs whilst also helping out now and again at the Carers Centre when time permitted. A hectic time it most certainly was, but I was enjoying every minute of it.

Going back in time briefly, I guess I've been my son's carer for about twenty-five years. I'm still counting and expect to continue my role for a little while longer yet. As I mentioned earlier, Chris's mum, Judith, and myself had decided to call it a day and we finally divorced in early 1997. It proved to be a trying marriage at times and Chris's hyperactive ways perhaps hadn't helped things too much along the way. Tensions at home were apt to suddenly boil over and Chris was occasionally in the mix of things. I had always felt that the marriage was an accident waiting to happen and when the final parting of the ways did come about it was thankfully on reasonably amicable terms. I feel that it's crucial for the normal development and happiness of children to see their parents being able to speak freely to one another with no animosity after a marriage break up.

So Chris and his sister, Hannah, were faced with a very difficult decision to make. Would they prefer to live with mum or dad following the divorce? I remember thinking at the time that they would probably struggle to make a quick decision as the outcome would prove to be so life changing for them. As things turned out, they made a rapid choice and they were united in their decision to remain with me. The eight-year-old spokesman Chris asserted, 'We're both in agreement that we want to stay with Dad. And that's our final decision.'

Frankly, I was thrilled to bits with this and I instantly felt all the built-up tension positively oozing out of me. And I soon realised I had acquired another new title for myself — a single dad!

As with numerous other people who find themselves in single-parent situations, I had no real perception of what to expect and what the future might hold in store for us once we officially became a family of three. Chris was always of special concern to me due to his growing list of foibles and unpredictable ways. As a single parent one unfortunately doesn't receive a textbook through the post telling one 'how to become a successful single parent in ten easy lessons'. Although it's one of the oldest cliches in the world, and I use it with a little reluctance, we really did take each day as it came and saw where that took us. Would Chris continue to have his tantrums and be as unpredictable as ever? Or could he become morose, introverted or withdrawn? And how would the tumultuous family upheaval impact on his behaviour at school — or Hannah's too for that matter? His early school years had already been up and down and evidence of learning issues was beginning to emerge. But thankfully, he was to become far more settled and much calmer. This obviously delighted me — it was an enormous weight off my mind. I was so relieved and thought to myself long may this all continue — for the sake of us all.

Role management inevitably was to become a delicate balancing act with the fundamental changes to our circumstances. I had to continue working full time but thank heavens for my employers' 'flexitime' initiative! My children were only eight and nine years old at the time and taking them to school by car in the mornings combined with somehow managing to pick them up *after* school became a tricky norm for a while and required plenty of organisation. Looking back, and everything considered, I think we handled those early days on our own fairly well overall and we didn't fall out very often. The three of us even managed a holiday break together in Majorca during summer school holidays which bonded us together even more. My children were clearly far more resilient than I had ever expected, or even hoped for.

I should add that even though we had been able to negotiate those first few hurdles successfully, if I had been able to wave a magic wand and teleport us forward twenty years in the blur of a few minutes and see glimpses of what the future had in store for us I can honestly say I have no idea how I would have felt. But I can well imagine.

I gradually became more familiar with carers and caring matters and started to learn a smattering of knowledge about the whole subject. I was asked by one of the managers at the Carers Centre if I would like to try my hand at speaking before invited groups of carers and professionals. All of these presentations would primarily be about my own caring story and journey, I was relieved to learn. You bet I'd have a go!

I wasn't sure where my new vein of confidence had come from but I was more than happy to go along with it while it lasted. Less than two years previously I would have been as nervous as a kitten if I was faced with similar circumstances. And that, if I was asked to speak in front of only two or three people!

I think I managed to negotiate my first test of public speaking reasonably well because no one said anything to the contrary. I discovered that by relating my own experiences along with other allied caring issues it proved energising and cathartic for me. And this would also appear to be the case from the feedback we received from listening consultants, doctors and nurses too. I learned that relating first hand stories, coming direct from active carers' mouths, is considered a powerful medium and thoroughly absorbed the professionals who listened.

The next sortie on my list of fundraising activities was to undertake the organisation of a live auction and the Carers Centre was happy for me to use their magnificent, newly revamped base as its venue. The predominant theme of the auction was Sports

Memorabilia, mainly football material. Collecting this sort of stuff has long been a big passion and interest of mine and I threw quite a few items from my own collection into the auction's melting pot. I managed to enlist the help of a small, but fantastic, team of helpers who supported me wonderfully throughout. The event would have been a near impossible task without their help and expertise. Over the course of about three months, we managed to gather together about four hundred attractive lots to be auctioned off, by an assortment of means. I even decided to try my hand at wielding the gavel and saved on the heavy cost of bringing in an auctioneer. The bidders and bids flew around everywhere as we finally got underway with arms shooting up seemingly everywhere. Although it was encouraging to come through it in one piece, I decided most definitely not to give up my day job! And at the first moment I was able to, I hung up my wooden gavel for all time.

I staged two auctions over the course of eighteen months and managed to raise a respectable combined total of £5,000 or so. We managed to attract interest from our local evening newspaper who were good enough to include features promoting the events and they published photographs of the more attractive lots. The newspaper coverage helped enormously to make the auctions successful. And as a direct result of their publicity, we were delighted to see that a good many more great quality donations rolled in through the doors for inclusion in our auctions.

It was around this time that my designated care liaison lady at the Carers Centre telephoned me, out of the blue, one afternoon. She informed me, with a little disguised excitement, that my name was included in the frame for winning that year's award of 'Carer of Year for the North West Region' of England. She implored me not to mention it to anyone for the time being as nothing had then been made official. My initial reaction was one of complete puzzlement. Why on earth could this be me? There are hundreds, maybe thousands of people, who do an equally good carers job and even a better one than myself. As instructed, I didn't dare tell anyone about this, other than my wife who is a paragon of discretion and I knew I could trust her implicitly to keep quiet. After all, the whole thing could have been well wide of the mark and I may have been confused with someone else. All kinds of thoughts entered my mind that evening. I was swimming in a unique mix of surprise, mystery, humbleness together with just a little dash of cautious excitement.

Later that week I was contacted again by the same person but this time I was asked if I could come over to the Carers Centre for a little chat 'about something'.

Whilst driving the three or so miles to the Centre I mulled over in my mind what all this mystery could be about. Being an eternal 'glass half full' type my mind was telling me the prestigious award that was hinted about earlier in the week could actually be genuine after all.

As it panned out, the news was even better than that. I had been confirmed as the winner of the annual Marsh Award for the Carer of the Year for the North West of England, one of eight UK regions in which winners were chosen. But in addition to this, I had also been nominated and was successful in landing the main award for the entire United Kingdom!

It was mind numbing and quite overwhelming. And, of course, it was incredibly humbling. I will say again that I felt sure that there had to be many more candidates from the four home countries that were far more suitable than myself to receive this accolade. But after my initial emotions had died down and the dust settled, I thought to myself, 'OK, I've somehow managed to land these fantastic awards, so I'm now going to try my best to really enjoy them. And I'll endeavour to do something really worthwhile in the following twelve months, in my carers capacity, to justify their faith in me.'

The Marsh Awards celebrate annually the outstanding contributions of people who are committed to social, cultural and environmental causes. The Trust, which was started by Mr Brian Marsh OBE in 1981, supports around 350 charities every year through the Grants Programme. It gives around 80 different Awards to individuals and groups from across the charity sector, who make a difference to a cause that they believe in.

The award presentation followed a few weeks later when an official from The Marsh Trust travelled up from London especially for the occasion. A nice, healthy cheque arrived and was handed to me together with framed Certificates and a couple of gifts, all of which made me feel incredibly proud. And a little wealthier as well. I was naturally expected to make some sort of acceptance speech which I managed to execute completely 'on the hoof' with zero notes or hints around to guide me. I remember precious little of what I said but I do have hazy recollections of one or two ripples of applause from the sizeable summer gathering. I can only assume, therefore, that my speech must have been reasonably well received.

I was determined to do the best I could in the next twelve months to keep the momentum going and maybe raise even more money if I could. I did not have any real forward plan of action but waited for a suitable opportunity to come about. I just decided to have a go at anything within the care sector, that might present itself in the months ahead. I was determined to try to make a difference, however small that difference was.

Later on during the same year I accepted an invite from the Lancashire & South Cumbria NHS Foundation Trust. They asked me whether I might be prepared to serve, as the Board's designated Carer Representative, on interview panels for vacancies which were likely to cover a broad range of nursing and senior management positions. I was naturally a little nervous at first but decided to give it my best shot. I was a little apprehensive asking questions to the applicants, because I wondered whether they were perfectly appropriate for the advertised position. But I have served on these panels now quite regularly for a few years so I feel reasonably comfortable about it all now.

In addition to helping out the Trust in a small way, I found that interviewing has helped me to develop my own knowledge of the internal and external workings of the health system. And, as with any help that I offer to the care and health sector, I do it entirely on a voluntary basis. I have always maintained that I would derive little pleasure and enjoyment if I was to receive any payment for care-related tasks that I took on. I am perfectly content with complimentary coffees and a couple of cakes — that's more than an adequate reward for me.

I did manage to complete another couple of fundraisers in the following year which took the running total of cash that was generated for the Carers Centre slightly over the £10,000 mark which was very pleasing.

A few months later, I learned from the Carers Centre staff that a team from BBC Radio Lancashire would be staging an outside broadcast direct from the Centre in the near future. I understood that the station's main presenter would be chatting live on the air to people who were connected to the Carers Centre to enable listeners to gain a better understanding of what us carers were all about. I was asked if I would be interested in being one of those people to have a short chat with the show's presenter. I didn't need to think about that one for too long at all. I responded in a mere twinkle of an eye, without any hesitation, 'Why not, yes please, count me in!'

I was, therefore, pencilled in as one of those scheduled to have a chat with the radio team along with other regular members of staff and a few active carers. Like all the others who had agreed to do this, I had no idea whatsoever the type of questions I was likely to be asked or what the discussion would entail. So I thought that rather than swot up for endless hours on topics that may not even be touched upon I decided, as usual, to do things my easier way and just simply 'wing it'.

The big day arrived and we found the radio team chatty and able to put us all at ease with friendly and quirky chatter before our respective spots took place. I can't for the life of me remember what I talked about but when it was over, I reckoned that my several minutes of glory may have been not too bad. I thought what a wonderful job it would be as a radio presenter if their days passed as rapidly as my little slot had!

I breathed a huge sigh of relief once it was all over, as I'm sure all the others did. I was about to gently tiptoe out the broadcasting room when one of the station's researchers glanced at me a little sternly and asked me if I would stay behind for a little while. A touch of real panic set in for the first time that day. What's this all about? Did I say something on the radio that sounded bad? Or was I controversial in some way and listeners had already started ringing in to complain? Did I accidentally swear on air as I suppose this could happen? Or did the whole thing just go horribly wrong?

It transpired that none of the above fears applied. The main presenter sauntered over and told me that he felt I had come over quite well and that I sounded 'natural enough'. We had a little chat about this and he asked whether I would like to visit their main studios in Blackburn and share a slot with him during one of his afternoon programmes. Wow! I was so excited that I felt like hugging him but I fell short of that thank goodness. Far from being reprimanded, or worse, for being rude or insulting on live radio they actually quite liked what they had heard!

So, they gave me a date to put in my diary and a few weeks later, I made the trip over to Blackburn for my first extended shot on live radio. It seemed to go reasonably well as no major hiccups were reported. I could hardly believe all the complex, technical equipment in the studio and felt a tinge of panic at the sight of it. I was relieved to learn, however, that all I had to do was to put on my headphones, position myself close to the large fluffy microphone, and do what I like doing most — simply natter! I talked about caring, carers and the Carers Centre and, overall, I was relaxed and felt well within my comfort zone. I seem to remember that I sneaked in a short 'hi' to Chris, whilst on the air, as he had promised me, he would tune in. Sadly, he was by now back on a Section 3 and, by a strange coincidence, he was based on a ward in Blackburn Royal Hospital, only about two miles away from the studio.

My trips over to Blackburn became a regular monthly date over the years and I am still invited to fill the occasional afternoon slot on Radio Lancashire to this day. I always feel a certain relaxed air of familiarity and friendliness whenever I am in the town. This may be due to the fact that my mother was born and bred there, before moving to Blackpool with my grandparents when she was nine years old.

So that is more or less where I am up to now. And I guess

that the caring world, in its many guises, continues to play a central role in my life. I wouldn't have it any other way and I am more than content with my lot at present and feel privileged that I can look after my son. When Chris finally gets his life firmly back on track and settles down to a better life in the community, I will undoubtedly continue to serve the caring community in my own small way.

I still deliver the occasional talk to one or two care groups in the Lancashire area which I always love to do and seldom refuse. For me, it serves the dual purpose of being able to share the caring gospel to a broader audience as well as helping to keep my own stress levels in decent running order and to stay well. I enjoy telling others about my own caring experiences and I usually add something to my repertoire each year as Chris invariably gets up to more and more tricks! I aim to tell everything exactly as it is — whether the times in question are good, bad, or indifferent.

My enthusiasm for all things 'caring' seldom wavers and, in the autumn of 2019, my zest was hugely reinforced when I was thrilled to receive a 'Local Hero' award from my own town, Blackpool. The initiative was set up to celebrate 125 years of the existence of Blackpool Tower. I am proud to be a Blackpudlian or 'Sandgrown'un' as we are traditionally known around these parts, so there could hardly be any better way to guarantee that I will stay well-motivated to the carers cause.

Latterly, I have enjoyed doing a fair amount voluntary work for the Blackpool Football Club Community Trust. These are largely activities with my 'carers hat' on. I find that my role with them is a 'win-win' situation because I am able to assist my football club in some way in addition to being able to assist people who suffer from various conditions such as social isolation, early onset dementia and depression. The Trust works to support local need and has worked with more than 25,000 Blackpool residents whilst delivering almost 14,000 sessions. It has invested £1.37m into the local community, engaging over 4,000 people each and every week. I have landed on my feet here and in a perfect capacity — and long may it all last!

So now, as we fast approach the end of this dreadful and unforgettable Covid-dominated year we are hopeful that next year will be a big year for Chris and, indeed, for everyone. Our main goal must be to find a way of preventing further relapses and to ensure that the subject of hospitals remain off limits for my son once and for all.

CHAPTER 7
RETURN TO THE PRESENT

It is late September 2017 and Chris has arrived back at the Harbour Hospital having just left his last port of call in Cheshire. It was not his first time at this hospital by any means. In fact, he had stayed on all three of the male wards at various stages in the past. He was already a familiar figure there and many of the staff knew him well. An ever-popular patient at the Harbour, they were pleased to have him back although I'm sure they would be keen to point out that it would have been preferable if he was not there at all — off his section and out of hospital.

He was allocated a bed on a familiar acute level ward. His move onto a less restrictive ward was encouraging news because he left behind a PICU ward in Cheadle and a step down was always regarded as very welcome news. The ward doctor at the Priory had worked wonders with Chris, and more than likely had sent reports over about the good progress he made while he was with them. I agreed wholeheartedly as I felt he had improved considerably in Cheshire; his treatment was excellent and he was in far better all-round shape than he had been for a long time.

What happened next at the Harbour was not quite so good, however. In fact, in my opinion a ridiculous decision was made which I will kindly describe as highly puzzling. He had been on his new ward only a matter of a week when he was told by the nursing staff that he was to be converted from Section 3 status to that of an 'informal' patient.

In this context, it could have meant either one of two things.

Firstly, an informal patient can be someone who has agreed to go into hospital for an assessment and treatment for a mental health disorder, The other meaning is the one which relates specifically to Chris. It can apply to someone who is detained under the Mental Health Act but their section has expired (a Section 3 needs to be extended each six months if it is deemed to be still necessary) and has not been renewed. One still has the same rights as those admitted to hospital with a physical condition and they can remain on the ward until alternative accommodation in the community can be arranged.

So what this meant in real terms was tantamount to Chris being switched overnight to the status of a voluntary patient. We were notified that he would be permitted to go outside the hospital grounds whenever he wanted to, within certain limits. The usual rules with regard to Section 17 leave, which he had adhered to for so long, would therefore no longer be applicable. He would also have free access to his personal money and have the freedom to make purchases. He suddenly discovered, much to his delight, that he was almost as free as a bird.

As a family, we didn't feel quite so elated, to put it mildly, when this surprise bombshell was unveiled. There are several other conditions that an informal patient can normally benefit from but the above one directly affected Chris. We were dumbfounded and thought to ourselves, 'Wow — how has he possibly made such a full and amazing recovery in the space of just seven days? If this is true, then it is a truly remarkable turn-around!'

Or could it be that an awful blunder had been made? I greeted the news with some incredulity. Of course, only time would now tell how things would pan out over the days and weeks to follow.

Chris was naturally thrilled to bits with the news. A whole new world — literally — had magically opened up before his eyes and he must have felt like a kid in a sweet shop. His first action after hearing the news was a trifle optimistic to say the very least. He asked the ward manager if he might now be able to leave the hospital immediately. He was quickly informed that his idea was a complete non-starter because he would first of all need to organise somewhere to live. And his care co-ordinator would undoubtedly attempt to block such a move unless a whole range of safeguards and a suitable care package were set up and put into place.

It would not have been possible for him to live with Sue and myself as we had long felt that this would lead to an enormous strain on our marriage. Chris never managed to fully get his head around this point or recognise the complications that his presence in the house could create.

All the above scenarios were rendered academic because Chris quickly messed everything up in a big way. In his infinite wisdom he decided to take periods of leave up to several times a day which in itself wasn't of any great concern to anyone. But it's what he got up to whilst outside of the hospital grounds that affected everyone — and especially himself.

We did stress to him on several occasions that if he could behave like a saint for a few more weeks once his informal status had become effective, he would have an excellent chance of winning himself a full discharge and be allowed to leave hospital completely. But, alas, he proceeded to badly abuse the fortuitous position that he had found himself in.

Once the wheels had been set in motion and he officially became an informal patient, it wasn't long at all before he was arriving back on the ward rolling drunk — and this happened on more than one occasion. He stayed out for a full day one day which caused more than a little concern for his ward's staff. He had access to all his money now but did not spend it wisely at all. Unshackled by the constraints he had been forced to endure over the previous two years he proceeded to throw money around like the end of the world was nigh. He even managed to procure some cocaine from somewhere while he was out on one of his jaunts and all these transgressions were carefully noted and ultimately resulted in a complete rethink at the hospital. So, after all the great work that the Priory hospital in Cheshire had achieved only weeks earlier, he now found himself almost back at square one. And, into the bargain, he was in one heck of a mental state yet again.

We felt it was so cruel for Chris, the ward staff and family alike. The episode had given him lots of hope that he would soon be freed and out of hospital. And it was cruel for us because all we could do was wait, hope and wonder what he was getting up to every day. He completely disregarded the fact that alcohol, dodgy substances and even high energy drinks, which he habitually used regularly, don't mix at all well with his complex concoction of prescribed medications.

As a result of all the bedlam and commotion he created, his Section 3 status was rapidly renewed for a further standard six-month period.

And to this very day we have no idea who was responsible for the decision not to immediately renew Chris's section in favour of allowing him an informal status. And no one there seemed particularly interested in owning up to it either!

Two weeks later Chris was up to his old tricks again and in a rebellious mood. Whilst out on 'hospital grounds leave' he eluded his escort and sprinted across the main Blackpool road and swiftly vanished from sight. This episode began on Monday 16 October and continued until late evening on the following day. He rang me almost straight away and said almost gleefully, 'Dad, I've escaped again. Don't worry, I'll be in touch probably in the next day or two.

In the next day or two! This part of his announcement really worried me. I lost count of the number of times he rang me after escaping and it sounded just as bad each and every time.

He contacted me several times during the time he was on the run but refused point blank to meet up with me. He was well aware, after all his previous breakouts, that I would make every attempt to have him returned safely to the hospital pronto by any means available. I did manage to ascertain from him that he had recently met a young lady and said that he would probably be 'staying over at her place'. But he kept her location strictly secret from me.

On day two, the police called at our house hunting for the usual clues as to his current whereabouts. I did reveal to them that he was keeping in regular touch and they asked me to listen carefully, if he rang again, for any tell-tale background noises which might help to determine where he was. But he was probably lying low at his new lady friend's house so noises such as the ping of a microwave were unlikely to yield much about where he was holed up.

That evening I watched my local team play Bury to help take my mind off the situation. I was no sooner sat in my usual seat when the public address system reported, 'This is a police announcement. If anyone knows the current whereabouts of Christopher Frowen, aged twenty-nine years, of Blackpool, or has any relevant information, would they please go to directly the players' entrance.'

The same message was broadcast again during the half time break and I closely watched the players' entrance for anyone who might be moving towards there.

I went to the match purely as an attempt to distract myself from Chris's situation and there it was blaring out to all and sundry! I was, of course, very grateful to the local police for their assistance but the appeal didn't seem to produce a result. I left the ground a long time before the end as there was a cold, biting wind, the football was of a dreadful standard and I was unable to get Chris out of my mind.

The moment I was back in the car, I decided to text Chris to tell him about the announcements in the ground and to plead for him to go back to hospital because this was starting to make us all feel ill.

I didn't receive a reply from him but I did receive a call from a member of staff on Chris's ward a while later who told me that he had returned to hospital voluntarily. Maybe my text appeal had somehow done the trick or perhaps was he ready to go back in any event?

Once back on the ward, Chris sensed that his two-day escapade had not gone down at all well. He did remain on that ward a little while longer until an unseemly incident resulted in his transfer to the more secure PICU environment. But the PICU ward at the Harbour was filled to capacity. So Chris had to move away again to the closest hospital that had a spare PICU bed available. A sheepish-sounding Chris rang me while in transit to say, 'I'm on my way to Blackburn Royal, Dad. And you don't want to know! I suppose there's worse places I could end up going to.'

'I'm sure you won't be there for long, Chris. And don't worry, I'll visit you lots. We'll soon have you back over here,' I replied with a dash of hopeful reassurance.

'Yeah, right. I'll believe that when I see it.'

By the middle of December, he was still in the psychiatric unit at Blackburn Royal Hospital at Pendle View. I was, at least, able to combine my visits with my scheduled slots on Radio Lancashire, as their studios are nearby in Blackburn's town centre. We had hoped that he may have managed to work himself a move back to Blackpool in time for Christmas but that prospect was looking bleaker by the day. The weather was also bleak over in east Lancashire. They had had heavy snow falls and there was some drifting in parts. But the deep snow and icy coldness did not prevent Chris from making yet another successful escape attempt. How he managed to abscond from their very secure PICU unit was way beyond me. His creative juices must have been operating on overdrive. It wasn't very funny really but I had to try to make light of this and similar absconding incidents or I may have ended up in a right old state!

As I recollect, it was early doors on a Friday evening when he ran off for about the twenty-fifth time in this dubious career of his. Had I kept a complete record of his 'running order' I'm sure it would have revealed that a high percentage of his escapes occurred on Friday evenings. He confided in me several times over the years that he felt he would be missing out on a decent night out with friends if he was left to 'vegetate on Friday evenings on my ward'. Curiously, he was inclined to phone me on Fridays to give me forewarnings of his intentions to make a bolt for it. I could never understand his logic with this. Why would he bother to tell me this when he simply had to know that the very next thing I would do, is to inform the ward staff to keep a very close eye on him for the remainder of the day?

I was notified that he had not returned to the ward and that the police had duly been informed. He didn't have much money with him by all accounts, it was a freezing cold evening, it was snowing heavily and he didn't have a coat on. I reckoned, therefore, that considering this unappetising combination there was a pretty good chance he would soon voluntarily return to the ward. That didn't turn out to be the case as he clung on to his freedom until almost midnight. He was finally located and picked up by our wonderful boys in blue — apparently numbed by the cold, shivering wildly and clutching a box of half-eaten KFC. And so, another absconding chapter was put to bed, thank goodness.

The Lancashire bed managers department had been kept busy with several requests to find Chris a suitable bed geographically closer to home. The efforts were eventually rewarded and, in early Spring, it was a welcome return to the Harbour for him. He hadn't shown much improvement in terms of either his health or behaviour during his time in Blackburn so he had to settle into a PICU bed again once he had arrived back 'home'.

He remained on the secure PICU ward until mid-summer. He hadn't been in trouble for months and, as there had been no attempts to abscond either, the family enjoyed a relatively peaceful period. But, to us, nothing appeared to be happening behind the scenes about the possibility of a rehabilitation placement which could eventually lead Chris to a further chance of living in the community. I recalled an old adage at the time — 'if there is no clear option then the best thing is to probably do nothing'. This struck a chord with me and I wondered whether the phrase was applicable to Chris's predicament.

It was at a crunch CPA meeting in early August that plenty of fur began to fly. As a family, we grew tired of being given bland promises of better things to come. I had made arrangements on this occasion to bring a few family members along with me to the meeting as I thought it might turn out to be a shrewd move. I reckoned that the more bite and incisiveness we might be able to input, the more likely it was that something positive could come out of it.

Whether it was a pure coincidence or not I will never know but it was only a matter of a few days later that Chris had moved into a rehabilitation unit in Brighouse, West Yorkshire!

I was normally the family's sole representative at CPA meetings and had attended something in the region of twenty such meetings over the years. This time I was delighted that Chris's mum, Hannah and her husband Gareth all agreed to join me in the fray. Hannah is a senior English teacher currently based in Dubai while Gareth recently passed his final exams to become a commercial airline pilot. The timing was fortunate for the two of them, and for me, because the school summer holiday period had begun and they were temporarily back in the country.

The usual tired spin about Chris's future was discussed in the early part of the meeting and then, at last, the worm turned. We began to question everything and give plenty back in return. Lots of searching questions were fired in salvos at the care professionals. They hadn't been used this level of assertiveness and argy-bargy before and it appeared that they became a little rattled. The meeting ended quite abruptly with only a minimum of pleasantries being exchanged. It seemed likely that what we had said managed to do the trick. Chris had his bags packed and was moved over to West Yorkshire.

It was sad that we had to resort to such extreme measures to simply speed up a fair deal for Chris. But past experiences had taught me that I shouldn't be surprised by this at all.

Cygnet Lodge is situated in the West Yorkshire town of Brighouse and is only two miles away from Wyke hospital, and this is where Chris was transferred to when he was first admitted to hospital during this current stretch. The unit is described as a high dependency inpatient rehabilitation service for men. Their emphasis is in preparing individuals for discharge or supporting those with longer term optimal functioning. It also provides the chance to evaluate what support a person may need on leaving hospital to help prevent readmissions and offers positive support.

It soon became clear to Chris after an initial meeting that his rehab stint could be set to last for up to a year. This was not what he had hoped for or expected at all. He imagined that a couple of months of rehabilitation might prove a long enough time to do the trick and to earn him a ticket out of hospital. As a result of this early disappointment, he sunk into low moods until he finally came to terms with the situation, at least to some degree.

He was told at his first meeting with senior staff that the first twelve weeks would be a period of initial assessment and the staff would then start to work actively on his needs with a specially tailored coaching programme. He didn't much like the sound of any of this either. He rang me after the meeting and yelled down the phone to me, 'What am I expected to do for three months, Dad? Just potter around doing nothing while they just stand around and gawp at me? It's just so stupid.'

I knew exactly where he was coming from and secretly, I was a little disappointed as well about this revelation. But I was certain that these good people knew exactly what they were doing and I gradually began to coax Chris around to my point of view.

Their psychologist and myself engaged in a number of telephone chats in the early weeks that Chris was there. He asked me many questions about his childhood, his schooling and he even expressed interest in his hobbies and other pursuits. This encouraged me a good deal and I was delighted to offer any help that I could if it was likely to speed up the whole process and result in a further early chance for him in the community.

I visited Chris at the Lodge once a week which was probably sufficient considering the distance involved. He was granted leave to walk around the town centre shops with me and we often went for a coffee together. An escort from the Lodge stayed glued to him the whole time as a safeguard in case he ever decided to do a runner. Maybe my son's past reputation for absconding had preceded him? He bought lots of items of designer clothing from a classy local shop with his 'benefit' cash that I electronically transferred over to him every two weeks. The shop owner wore a beaming smile each time Chris breezed in knowing full well that money would soon be flying around like confetti. It was now eight weeks into his time in Brighouse and Chris was starting to feel slightly more settled after all the early disappointments.

Nothing, however, is ever too settled in Chris's life as we have seen many times before. And he was up to his mischievous tricks again before long. He ran away from his escort on one occasion while out on an hour's leave. He did return to the unit voluntarily an hour later, thus limiting the damage he caused to himself in terms of future leave allowances. I never learned about this minor absconding sortie from the staff and I remained blithely oblivious to it. I could sense that something more substantial was starting to bubble up in Chris — call it a father's intuition, if you like. I wasn't really sure what this was all leading up to but it wasn't long before I found out.

My intuition proved to be accurate on this occasion, although I took no pleasure whatsoever from that. It was a Friday — yet again — and he was evidently itching for a spot of weekend fun. He managed to escape from the unit with consummate ease and quickly disappeared. Cygnet Lodge is situated high above the town in a district called Raistrick and he nonchalantly wandered down into the town and entered a nearby local pub. He spent an hour or two there relaxing without a single care in the world. It was early November and the day quickly turned to night. I was informed that he had absconded but I was becoming so accustomed to this sort of thing that I simply sat calmly at home and waited for him to contact me or for further updates from the Lodge or from the local police. There was no further need for mid-afternoon tots of whiskey for me!

He did ring me at about 6pm and I noticed that he sounded a little drunk. He said that he was sorry for what he had done but felt he needed some time out on his own. I thanked him for letting me know that was safe but gently suggested that it would be for the best if he returned to base now that he had had a few hours of fun. He replied with, 'bye, Dad' and hung up. I wondered what else he had up his sleeve for the evening.

I found out an hour later when I received a surprise phone call from a taxi driver with a broad Yorkshire accent who said to me through a crackly line, 'Hello, I have your son in my taxi and he wants me to take him to Blackpool. He has no money. Will you be able to pay me yourself when we reach your house, please? He says you always have lots of money.'

'I don't want you to take him to Blackpool because he has to stay in Brighouse. And I don't have lots of money anyway!' I replied without wanting to elaborate much about Chris's circumstances.

'It's a bit late for that, mate, because we are already on the M62 motorway and heading west in your direction — and fast!'

I immediately resigned myself to the fact that Chris would

be arriving outside my house in a West Yorkshire taxi cab in about an hour and a half. I couldn't think of anything else to say to the driver other than, 'Well, how much is all this going to cost me then?'

'Ninety-five quid, mate.'

'What! Can you not turn around at the next junction and return to Brighouse?' I asked him in a stunned voice more in hope than anything else.

'Not a chance, mate, because I won't get paid anything then'.

I realised I was getting nowhere fast with this line of conversation so I decided to give up.

'OK, I suppose I'll see you in an hour or so then.'

I rang Chris on his own phone. He told me excitedly that they had reached the M61 motorway and he would be back in Blackpool in about forty-five minutes. He was completely oblivious to the seriousness of his predicament; all he could envisage was an opportunity to have a fantastic weekend away in Blackpool and see his beloved Tower again.

Sue and I watched anxiously at the window for a Yorkshire taxi to pull up outside our house. I was ready with cash in hand as I saw Chris alighting merrily from the cab. I asked the driver if I could have a receipt for the money and he duly obliged. I'm not sure now why I bothered to go to the trouble of obtaining this. Maybe I would show it to Chris one day when he was in a better place and ask him for a full reimbursement?!

It was 7.30pm as Chris marched into our house. He told us he had hardly eaten a thing since lunchtime so Sue made him a snack whilst I made him a strong black coffee, which I felt he badly needed. As he tucked in, I strongly suggested that he really must return to Brighouse tonight and stressed that he was still on a Section 3. I also pointed out that the two of us would also be breaking the law if we allowed him to stay at our house. A heated discussion followed which resulted in Chris storming out the house and melting away into the Blackpool night.

I now needed to make phone calls — and fast. Firstly, I informed Cygnet Lodge that Chris had found his way back to Blackpool, for which they thanked me. I then rang the local police station who were already well familiar with my son's escaping antics over the years. The operator told me they would send a car with two officers and they would be with us soon.

I was already on first name terms with the officers as they had called at our house on other occasions for the very same reason. I often wondered what our neighbours thought each time police cars arrived outside our house. I was told to inform the police if Chris returned to our house, by quoting the specially allocated reference number they gave me. Or if he rang and offered us any indication as to his whereabouts, I was to let them know details without delay. The officers also asked for the names and addresses of any friends that he may visit and I suggested that they might focus their attention on one of his mates in particular. And it was this friend who eventually was to provide the key to his whereabouts. A few hours passed by and the police now knew that he was somewhere in an area of Bispham, to the north of the town. His friend's parents had tipped off the police as to the approximate area that the pair of them might be.

The panic was finally over shortly after midnight when Chris, by then all alone and more than likely nursing a headache, was picked up by police on Blackpool's north Promenade as he trudged back from Bispham.

What a Friday evening that was! We had made plans to go out with a few friends but that had to be put onto the back burner, at very short notice, until a later date.

His journey back to West Yorkshire was a co-ordinated two-car affair. Our Lancashire police apparently drove him as far as the border where they were met by a West Yorkshire police car who took him the rest of the way. And with that, one of Chris's more colourful and, for me, expensive escape episodes had finally drawn to a close.

A few weeks later Chris's short dalliance with rehabilitation at Cygnet Lodge came to a sudden and inglorious end. He had never truly settled there and had not fully recovered from his ill-advised excursion to Blackpool. Chris has always been prone to sudden bouts of anger although these often subside as quickly as they erupt. An altercation had evidently developed in the unit's lounge area between him and another patient. Chris may have been in a red mist as he tempestuously ripped a large flat screen television from its wall mounting and hurled it to the ground, smashing it beyond repair. Not surprisingly, this proved to be the final straw for the Lodge and within twenty-four hours he was all packed up again and hastily despatched to the Harbour. And in view of the enormity of his final parting shot in Brighouse it was back to a PICU ward for Chris. And, at the same time, it was back to the drawing board.

December and January were good months for Chris at the Harbour; he settled down well and his behaviour was described as excellent. He always responded well to the lower stimulus atmospheres the PICU wards afforded him and it was no exception this time. The number of patients on these wards are generally quite a lot lower than on acute wards and the staff are, therefore, able to devote more time and attention to each patient.

By the end of January 2019, Chris had done so well that he was stepped down to the acute Orwell ward where he had already been before. He was now back in settled mental shape and as healthy as he had been for ages. In fact, he was so well that it was being widely discussed amongst the professionals that he could be given another chance to leave hospital in the near future if he maintained or improved this level of progress. A minor hiccup did occur, however, after a consultant temporarily suspended his Section 17 leave. The decision was based on Chris sneaking in an occasional can of beer whilst he was on leave, the odour on his breath easily giving the game away. The ward staff also noted that he brought back a packet of disposable razors although there was never any suggestion that he intended to use them for any reason other than for shaving. Chris was annoyed about the razor incident as he felt it was treated unfairly and it was a complete injustice. He rebelled in his own tried and trusted fashion — by absconding for a full day (purely as a personal protest, he told everyone at the time). But this single blip apart, he received great reviews and feedback from his nursing staff.

Chris's care co-ordinator, and the Forensic Services, who provide treatment for persons with severe and disabling mental disorders in conditions of therapeutic safety, had worked together for months, in determined attempts to break the impasse and get Chris's life back on track. The UBU, which I mentioned earlier in the book, was overseeing the possibility of Chris moving to their assisted accommodation facility in Lytham St Annes. Two senior representatives from the UBU met with Chris at the Harbour and left him feeling reasonably content with his general mental health and presentation. They felt he was 'borderline' suitable at that stage for a discharge into their facility. They did feel it necessary to continue meeting with him to monitor his progress on an ongoing basis.

Our family were quite excited with the news that his long

term in hospital may soon be drawing to a close. Chris was granted one full afternoon leave session each week so that he was able to visit his proposed new abode. The flat had been newly refurbished to an excellent standard, and he was more than happy to visit regularly and familiarise himself with all the facilities.

I met up with two of the UBU management staff several times and we shared views about Chris at some length. I was obviously still very keen for him to be given another chance to prove himself but I was beginning to have one or two reservations of my own. It was clear that the UBU people were also having a few doubts themselves about suitability. It was beginning to look like Chris's hopes of a move out of hospital were on the wane.

He made trips over to St Annes by bus and was allowed to travel unescorted. He did have an occasional alcoholic drink en route to St Annes which didn't go unnoticed by the UBU people. But in view of his length of time in hospital they glossed over this to a large extent. But Chris spoke freely to the UBU people about his continuing interest in cocaine and other similar unpleasant substances. It was this revelation that finally put the tin lid on any chance of the elusive discharge he had hoped for. The staff at UBU quite rightly felt that there was a very good chance he would soon be seeking out illegal substances if the move was allowed to go ahead.

It was all so very sad. So near and yet so far. Everyone had tried so hard and done their very best — the ward staff, the UBU people, forensic services and the family — to get a freedom show on the road but, in the final reckoning, there was only one person who was in a position to scupper the whole thing.

Chris remained on the same ward until early June. His standard of behaviour had been up and down since the UBU debacle and a couple of further abscondings happened in the meantime. He returned each time on his own accord but he had clearly been under the influence of some substance on each occasion. It was also reported that he was becoming increasingly bolshy while on the ward. These incidents, one by one, started to stack up and eventually culminated in the decision to transfer him again to a PICU ward to give him time to stabilise and cool off.

But again, there were no spare beds available in the Harbour's PICU ward and Chris was forced into moving away again. I sometimes wondered why he ever went to the inconvenience of unpacking his bags and cases when he was required to fill and empty them with almost ridiculous regularity.

The next stop on his travels took him to a hospital called Bartle Priory, which is fifteen miles away from Blackpool and four miles from Preston. It is set in beautifully scenic grounds deep in the Fylde countryside. Bartle Hall, which is an 18th century manor house set in many acres of landscaped gardens, is only a matter of a few hundred metres away. One might imagine then that Chris could have a reasonably calm time while he was there and it did go well for several weeks. But an incident on his ward at the end of his stay proved quite traumatic for Chris and he was on his way again.

It was now the middle of summer and we were in the middle of a decent spell of warm weather. I was able to cycle the round trip of thirty miles to The Priory a few times each week as it was so pleasant. Hannah was back in the country again for her summer break and the two of us enjoyed scenic drives in the countryside each time we visited Chris.

One Saturday in mid-August, seven weeks after Chris had first landed at Bartle Priory, a very disappointing absconding episode occurred. This one was particularly annoying because it should never have happened. It came about as a direct result of Chris being handed all his available cash in one instalment by the ward staff. The sum involved amounted to about £100.

I had earlier implored the staff not to allow him to have more than small amounts of money at any one time, especially when he was set to go on a period of leave. I outlined the reasons that were based on many earlier experiences that had gone awry and stressed how vital it was for them to adhere to this. I emphasised that the temptations for him would simply be too great. And to make things a little worse still, by this stage he was given unescorted leave.

The inevitable outcome did come about and he blew all his cash in one single day. He failed to return from his leave and somehow managed to hire a taxi, out in the wilderness of the countryside where the hospital was. The cab driver took him to Blackpool, which immediately set him back £35. Had he considered that it would cost him a similar amount later for his return trip to the hospital, I wondered? Little is known of his whereabouts as he roamed around Blackpool (he certainly didn't contact me at any time during this sortie) but we did discover that he managed to obtain a batch of cocaine and, no doubt, 'enjoyed' it whilst he was out on the town. He was eventually spotted by police in the town centre late in the evening after they received an alert and was subsequently returned to the hospital. And happily, yet another 'escape' had reached a safe conclusion.

I learned most of the details of his adventure in Blackpool from Chris himself the following morning. Far from sleeping off all the previous day's activities, I discovered that he was wide awake and had been unable to sleep all night. This was clearly due to the continuing effects of the cocaine which linger for days. I had a real go at the staff for acting in direct opposition to my strong advice. They promised me faithfully that if he was ever granted leave again the same situation would definitely not arise.

I was still so annoyed about what had happened the previous evening and also because Chris would now not have any money to spend for the whole of the following week. And I would then have to 'sub' him if he was desperately in need of something.

I am not permitted to say in any detail what took place on my son's ward that same afternoon due to the nature of what took place, and at the time of writing was not concluded. Let it suffice to say that there was a nasty incident and, as this impacted on my son's immediate future at Bartle, I feel obliged to mention it in the very briefest of terms. Chris was upset with what had happened and I promised I would take every step possible to get him transferred as soon as possible, if that was what he wanted. I really hoped that he would be able to sleep that night, notwithstanding the lingering after-effects of his cocaine binge the night before and due to the incident earlier on.

I telephoned Bartle Hospital the following morning and spoke to Chris first of all to see how he was feeling and whether he had managed to get much sleep. He was subdued which did not really surprise me. I then spoke to a senior member of their staff and stated that I would like to request a transfer as soon as convenient because Chris was now unsettled there.

Within twenty-four hours I was informed by the ward manager at Bartle that Chris was set to be transferred to the Harbour later in the day. She was apologetic about the way everything had turned out for Chris during his time there and wished him the very best with his recovery.

It was a pleasant change this time to see Chris back at the Harbour. He was put onto a different acute level ward to his previous one there and they were made aware of the circumstances that surrounded Chris's transfer back and treated him accordingly.

He told me that his initial thoughts as he passed through the double doors of his new ward were, 'I hope this ward turns out to be as lucky as the last time I was on here, Dad.'

'Yes, all fingers and toes crossed you're right with that, Chris,' I responded because I knew exactly to what he was referring.

Back in the autumn of 2015 it was on this ward, at a CPA meeting, that he was officially discharged from his Section 3 and moved into his new flat. And to this day, it remains the last occasion that he has been discharged from a mental health section.

As it turned out, Chris's stay on his new ward lasted little longer than a few weeks. But unlike on the previous joyous occasion, he moved only to his more familiar acute ward, not, alas, via the exit door and into the world outside. He did manage to squeeze in one more successful escape episode in the brief time before he switched wards. He was once again handed a substantial amount of cash that I had left on the ward with specific instructions to be gradually 'drip fed' to him. I expressly begged the staff not to give him more than about £10 at any one time. The anticipated outcome came about yet again and he tottered back onto the ward much later rather intoxicated.

This was his umpteenth time that Chris had been placed on his current ward and in many ways, it felt like we were coming back home. But, as always, I hoped that his stay there would be brief and we could somehow manoeuvre a legitimate passage out of hospital once and for all.

The weeks and months in the latter part of 2019 faded away with no other bad incidents of any note. With a mixture of the good relationships he enjoyed with staff members on the ward, and the warm feeling of being home in Blackpool with his family nearby, Chris entered the new decade with a justifiable feeling of renewed hope.

Chris's settled spell continued well into the new year and he was rewarded with periods of unescorted leave off the hospital grounds but unlike several times in the past, he used his time off the ward sensibly and no bad incidents were reported. I was told that he brought back several bits and bobs of food shopping and essential items of clothing but there was nothing that might be termed dodgy. What a refreshing change it was to hear waves of positive feedback wafting over from the ward staff many times over! Maybe my optimistic take about Chris and the new decade would become a reality after all and not be just a pipe dream.

There would be no party for Chris's thirty-second birthday in March because the Covid-19 lock-down had become effective during the same week. Sue and myself were able to meet him but in the hospital car park and only briefly at that. We were able at least to wish him a 'happy birthday' but only through the closed windows of the car and left his presents outside the car. He couldn't fully understand why we were unable to give him big hugs and see him '100% in person'. It was sad but absolutely necessary in view of Sue's vulnerability and our need to remain super-cautious.

Three key unrelated events occurred soon afterwards and had the effect of derailing Chris's progress quite badly. Firstly, as stated above, he was only able to see us on his birthday through a closed car window and he would not see me — or any of his family — again for many more weeks until after he had been transferred to yet another hospital in July. The Harbour's policy of not admitting visitors at the time was clearly the correct policy given the worsening virus situation. Secondly, his unescorted leave had to be stopped due to the risk of spreading the virus and the lock-down. He was proud of what he had achieved in terms of his behaviour since the turn of the year and his leave had been taken away from him through no fault of his own. He had difficulty accepting this and was upset and irritated for some time afterwards. And then worst of all, his grandpa, whom he adored, died suddenly and unexpectedly and this had a major impact on him.

The combined factors conspired against Chris and resulted in him being somewhat truculent on the ward. No one seemed too bothered to find out the reason why his behaviour had suddenly taken a marked downwards dip. He is inclined, by his very nature, to bottle things up when bad things happen and this was clearly one of those times. One lunchtime soon after he stabbed a cutlery knife into a chair in the dining area in sheer anger and frustration. It was this incident that brought about his swift transfer to a PICU ward again. It is such a shame that the ward staff were unaware of his personal circumstances at the time because this decisive action may not have been necessary at all.

And then surprise, surprise — the Harbour's PICU ward had no spare beds available again. Chris had to move away to a different hospital for the umpteenth time. We had been so optimistic that he would be given another shot at living in the community sometime in 2020. A 'less restrictive placement' was the term bandied about by his care co-ordinator and consultant. His behaviour had been very good, he was fully compliant with his medications and he had made his own determined efforts to rid himself of the urge to take drugs effectively up to this point. But a single cutlery knife stabbed into a chair had intervened in his future.

He was set for another stretch at Cygnet Wyke in Yorkshire again... or was he? He was transported to his new abode in Yorkshire, a familiar place to him already from a few years previously. But his stay there was destined not to last. In fact, the length of his time there could receive a worthy nomination in the Guinness Book of Records as the shortest stay ever for a patient in a Mental Health facility! He had scarcely stepped inside the hospital when he was informed that there was no longer any bed available for him. Chris rang me at this point and told me he was now past caring about anything and I fully appreciated how he would be feeling. So when he was told that he would be taken straight away to Darlington in County Durham he simply shrugged his shoulders and said in a resigned tone,

'OK, whatever — let's get on with it then.'

I was incensed when I found out about this latest shenanigan. What on earth was going on? Three hospitals in the space of less than twenty-four hours? This really was a bit much even for Chris in his current hospital-hopping marathon tour.

Our family of four once lived in the north east of England. Well, for about four years anyway, as I outlined in an earlier chapter. I always loved the people up there for their warmth and good natures. So I could somehow sense in advance that he would be treated well in Darlington. His new home, for significantly longer than twenty-four hours we hoped, is called Cygnet Victoria House. It is a twenty-five-bed mental health inpatient service for men. It's well regarded as a 'safe and stabilising environment for men who are experiencing an acute episode of mental illness and require emergency admission'.

I somehow knew that Chris would land on his feet in Darlington even though the opportunity had come about fortuitously. It was a pleasant surprise to hear one of their staff report that he felt comfortable almost straight away. One major factor in his favour was the fact that he was allowed to smoke fairly freely there which pleased him no end. And the staff were fantastic with him. Nothing was too much trouble he often told me. Their psychologist took the time and trouble to conduct a series of tests with him and the results proved to be extremely useful — and encouraging too. She spoke to me on several occasions to seek out historical information about Chris especially concerning his school life. The ward staff were also keen to engage Chris in afternoon occupational therapy sessions which he enjoyed and clearly proved beneficial to his well-being. He felt valued and important whilst at Victoria House and his mental health improved considerably as a result.

His main nurse, who was wonderful throughout his stay, said to me during one of our many telephone conversations that 'sometimes it's worth taking a risk with a patient and seeing how he would fare in the community especially when it's been such a long, long, time'. This single sentence resonated with me so much and boosted me no end. I felt buoyed by this positive and bold statement. Perhaps we were now firmly on the right path, I was left to conclude.

Chris's contentedness and the boost to his self-esteem were particularly important at the time as he was a hundred miles away from home and he hadn't seen any of his family for more than three months. It was long way for me to travel to visit but I certainly would have made the journeys had I been allowed to. But the 'no visitors' policy was still in force everywhere due to virus restrictions so the most we could manage was to 'see' each other whilst using the Skype and WhatsApp apps.

Since the turn of the year Chris and I had read books to each other over the phone during our evening conversations. After all, when one speaks to someone every day, and very often more than once a day, there are bound to be occasions when it's a struggle to find something new to talk about. Some of his main interests include Doctor Who, which he has always been fanatical about, the singers Cher Lloyd, Cheryl Tweedy (or whatever she is called these days) and latterly Ariana Grande — and also a yearning for king-sized kebabs! But we couldn't continue to talk about these topics for indefinite periods. So as we had been unable to see each other for months on end due to the pandemic we hit on this book reading idea and it proved to be a big success.

I used to read quite often to both my children at bedtimes when they were young but in those days, I made the stories up as I went along and narrated to them straight 'off the cuff'. I invented a theme about a family of six foxes who got up to all manner of mischief on their travels. Hannah has said to me many times since those days that I should write a book about the foxes' escapades which they found hilarious once upon a time and I may well surprise her one day! I'm sure many readers will agree that it's fairly easy to make up stories when children are young as they seldom notice the odd mistake or discrepancy that sometimes sneaks into the stories.

Chris's reading ability has improved greatly in recent times and he simply loves to be praised when he correctly pronounces a 'big word' that he hasn't seen or heard before. Maybe his sudden literary improvement is a further example of him beginning to exorcise the memories of inferiorities that blighted his childhood. His progress in this area may also be largely due to his ADHD medication (Atomoxetine) which was prescribed in recent times. His attention and concentration levels have clearly improved significantly since then.

Everything changed suddenly when, out of the blue one

morning, Chris rang me to say he was on the move again. He said that he was going 'somewhere closer to home' but he didn't know exactly where to. It has always been hospital's policy to return patients closer to their homes and families whenever possible but I had mixed feelings about this new development. It would obviously be great to have Chris back with us somewhere in Lancashire but he had made such significant strides forward in Darlington and in such a short period of time. I feel that, more than likely, he would have continued to improve even more if he'd had the opportunity. It was now late in June 2020 and I would, therefore, reserve judgement about this new transfer until I learned exactly where his next port of call would be.

Chris made the cross-Pennine trek from Darlington to Ormskirk District General Hospital. The hospital is, technically, just inside the Lancashire border but still forty or so miles from Blackpool via motorway links. We were breaking in new ground here as Chris had landed at one of the few north west hospitals that he hadn't visited before. His stay in Ormskirk was destined only to be for about seven weeks and I must say that the staff on his ward did a pretty good job in often tricky circumstances. Chris reverted to a rocky roller-coaster spell of several ups and downs whilst he was there.

Shortly after his arrival, having unpacked his stuff in another new room, he rang me to tell me disconsolately, 'I can't smoke here, Dad. It's gonna be absolutely crap. Can you do something about it please?'

'I'm afraid it's now the policy under new NHS rules that smoking is banned anywhere inside hospital grounds, Chris,' I replied factually but it was hardly likely to be of any help to him.

'It's so stupid. I could smoke as much as I wanted to yesterday in Darlington so what's the big difference now just a day later?' he moaned.

'I know, Chris, it's not good is it. I'll have a word with the staff once you've settled yourself in,' I replied, knowing only too well that there would be precious little that I would be able to do to improve things for him.

It does seem crazy, on the face of it, that a patient can be transferred from one hospital to another and may have to go through an immediate 'cold turkey' process at the new place with the consequence of suffering mental and physical torture. I am a non-smoker myself but I do know from personal experiences that if Chris is deprived of tobacco for any length of time his mood and general conduct soon degenerate very significantly. Does this mixed smoking policy have a positive impact on a patient and speed up his recovery, I ask? I'll leave you to decide the answer to that one…

I travelled to see him two days after he had arrived at Ormskirk and it was a special visit. We had previously not been apart for more than a week in the past and it was fifteen weeks since we had last met. Even though we spoke daily, sometimes several times, we had so much to talk about during this actual 'real meeting'. The only blot on the landscape was when he sank into gloomy spells as he complained bitterly about being unable to satisfy his nicotine needs.

Chris was permitted to smoke whilst outside the hospital grounds and, a few weeks after his arrival, he was thrilled to be granted periods of escorted leave outside of hospital grounds. He caught up hugely with his nicotine fixes then — he even bought himself some massive cigars, no doubt as a swipe at the authorities and as a personal symbolic gesture!

Shortly before his brief spell at Ormskirk drew to a close, he was given unescorted leave with me. It was always a better kind of leave because, even though escorts were unobtrusive and kept a fair distance away to allow us a modicum of privacy, we now had free reign, within reason, to go wherever we wanted. He did take some liberties with me that he would never have attempted with a staff member. He had a habit of popping into off licences for cans of beer which annoyed me hugely. It was always difficult for me when this kind of thing happened because if I were to create about it too much, he would become angry very quickly indeed and sometimes threatened me with running away. And when I escorted him back to the ward in a slightly inebriated state it hardly reflected too well on me either. But he came through his spell at Ormskirk with no absconding episodes documented and his reputation remained intact.

And then on 20 August Chris rang me excitedly to tell me that he was on the move again.

I had a very good idea why he was so euphoric this time. The news was very welcome indeed as you will discover in the next, and final, chapter.

CHAPTER 8
THE FUTURE IS HERE

Kemple View is a ninety-bed service which is managed by the Priory Group and caters for the needs of male patients with mental health and/or personality disorders. Their aim is to maximise opportunities for recovery, rehabilitation and independent living. It is situated in Langho in Lancashire, with Blackburn close by. And it's also only about twenty-five miles away from Blackpool which is very handy for me.

The likelihood that a rehabilitation placement would be made available to Chris had bubbled along on the agenda for quite some time and it has been an exciting prospect for him and for us all. But we have always said to ourselves — 'we'll believe it when we actually see it happen'. And who could blame us for being just a little wary and cynical after all the ups and downs we've been through?

Well, it has finally come about at long last. The wheels had been set in motion some time ago for Chris to have a rehabilitation placement at Kemple View but we remained cautiously guarded in our optimism. There was the ongoing Covid-19 pandemic to take account of and the endless uncertainty which surrounded it. And this point was especially relevant in view of the fact that the hospital is situated only a few miles from Blackburn where infection levels were consistently very high.

Additionally, Chris's behaviour was always a possible cause of concern. If his mental health or conduct had taken a dip during the course of the year then it's possible that the offer could have been withdrawn. But he buckled down and did extremely well and deserved his chance. As the saying goes, all the ducks are now in a line and we hope that they continue to waddle along on a straight path until we reach the end of the road.

Chris has been given an assurance that should his time at Kemple View ultimately prove successful then he will have earned himself another shot of freedom in the community. And that would present him with a perfect opportunity to get his life back on track at long last. I continue to remind him that he is now on the very top rung of the ladder and his quest for freedom and good mental health is now well in sight. All we have to do is to avoid the risk of meeting any snakes that might send him sliding back down again.

Kemple View is part of the Priory group and specialises in rehabilitation and recovery for people who need stable and safe services that are situated within a broader but focused pathway of care towards rehabilitation. The patients they care for often come from a diverse range of services where there has been placement breakdown due to severe and enduring mental health behaviours. These patients can typically be ones who are moving across from acute mental health wards or other mental health services which have struggled to deliver improvements in outcomes.

In 2019, Kemple View was successful in being rated 'outstanding' by the health and social care watchdog, the Care Quality Commission (CQC). It received an 'outstanding' rating in all five assessment categories: 'safe', 'effective', 'caring', 'responsive' and 'well-led'.

By being rated 'outstanding' overall, and in all categories, it joined the highest rated specialist mental health services in

England. This presents Chris with the perfect opportunity to achieve good and long-lasting health.

Early indications suggest that Chris is beginning to settle into his new place fairly well. He is not allowed to smoke which is causing him a little grief but in the fullness of time this may turn out to have a silver lining. It is already noticeable, after only three months, that during our telephone conversations we are hardly ever interrupted by intermittent fits of coughing and spluttering. His lungs are clearly recovering all the time and long may this last and improve even more.

He was originally led to believe that his placement might last for a period of twelve weeks — or a little less than that if he fully engaged with the staff and psychologists in all sessions and activities. It is now apparent, from what we have heard since his arrival, that his stay may continue for a period of twelve to eighteen months. The revelation has not enthralled him to put it very mildly but I understand that the hospital has a devoted and skilled team who are well accustomed to dealing with these types of issues and I have every confidence in them.

As I have stated earlier, he has been unsuccessful in his two previous rehabilitation attempts. These ended badly and abruptly and they may have been examples of the wrong places at the wrong times. He is now several years older, a little more mature and wiser and, arguably, in a far better position overall to handle the demands that will be placed upon him. So we live in eternal hope that this will be a case of third time lucky!

I would never dream of setting out what I think Chris will need to do to remain out of hospital once his rehabilitation programme has been completed and he has been discharged from the service. This is the responsibility of the professionals who are infinitely better placed than myself to deal with this side of things. A couple of points do seem certain to me though. He will need to have a good, solid, comprehensive package of care in place and plenty of close monitoring for an extended period of time following his discharge into the community. And he must conquer, once and for all, the substance misuse issues that have fundamentally undermined his recoveries in the past. And additionally, on the same subject, it would be highly desirable if he could ditch the cluster of friends who have aided and abetted him in the past, albeit largely unwittingly, and got him into this fine old mess in the first place.

And when his Mental Health section does finally draw to a close, I will be on hand, as always, wherever and whenever I may be needed to give him the parental guidance and help, he will more than likely need from time to time.

As we are fast reaching the end of my story it is now December 2020 and yet another obstacle has been tossed in our direction. I learned that Chris tested positive for Covid-19 and was placed in isolation for a while. Fortunately, he experienced only mild symptoms and has since fully recovered. Surely, if anyone deserves another chance in life it has to be my son!

Nelson Mandela once famously said, 'After one has been in prison it is the small things that one appreciates.' Technically, Chris hasn't been in prison but I'm sure the above sentence will resonate powerfully with him once this is all over. And it obviously goes without saying that it will be wonderful when we do finally reach the end of our long and winding road.

And who knows, at journey's end, we may see a road sign that will read 'Utopia — welcome to the future, Chris'.

END

At a theme park with his sister in 1993. And both proudly wearing their Blackpool FC shirts!

2010. Just home from an outward-bound day in the Lake District as part of his Princes Trust experience. And still with his war paint on!

Hot off the Press! A rare
meet up at Kemple View
in April 2021

Early July 2020 at
Ormskirk Hospital. A
happy Chris at our first get
together for months due to
the Covid pandemic.

With a proud dad looking down wondering what life has in store for young Christopher James Robert Frowen.

Just the two of us on holiday in Spain in 2004 at another theme park

A day out at a Doctor Who exhibition. Chris looks delighted to be inside the Tardis!